INTERNATIONAL PRAISE FOR
INSIDE THE KINGDOM

"Perhaps the most vivid account yet to appear in the West of the oppressive lives of Saudi women . . . She has emerged from her ordeal with some urgent insights into the kingdom from which she escaped . . . Let's hope that more brave dissenters—male and female—will follow her lead."

—*Wall Street Journal*

"To stand up as a woman and share her personal experiences and feelings . . . is surely a bold and possibly consequential act. Bin Ladin's memoir gives us an additional perspective on the Saudi world . . . A painful picture."

—*USA Today*

"A rare look [from] the only family member to talk openly about Osama Bin Laden."

—Associated Press

"Takes us into the heart of the ruling class of Saudi Arabia, and into the Bin Laden tribe . . . The Middle Ages in the desert with dollars added . . . She fled the clan, fought to save her children, publicly condemned Osama, and criticized Saudi Arabia: that's a lot."

—*Le Figaro*

"Carmen Bin Ladin chronicles her nine years of married life in a puritanical, male-dominated community where 'women are no more than house pets' . . . The book is a diary-style account of her struggle to cope with rules and strictures as suffocating as the desert climate."

—*International Herald Tribune*

more . . .

"[Carmen Bin Ladin] reveals the literally veiled life she led."
—*U.S. News & World Report*

"Tells how she fell in love with the rich Saudi Arabian that she met in Geneva, and how, after the early days of happiness, she had to face the reality of life within a powerful Saudi family . . . Today she has chosen to tell the truth . . . For her it is the only way to fight against the terror."
—*Paris Match*

"INSIDE THE KINGDOM traces her marriage's bitter unraveling, along the way providing a fascinating account of what it's like to live in the world's strictest Muslim theocracy . . . [Bin Ladin's] fairness, cultural sensitivity, and admiration for some of her Saudi relatives strengthen her story. This is not a vengeful tell-all but rather a woman's courageous tale of emancipation by way of choosing freedom over intolerance."
—*Time Out New York*

"Bin Ladin details the oppression of women in Saudi Arabia and within the Bin Laden clan."
—*TIME*

"Startling . . . A dire prophecy regarding the future of western culture . . . [A] warning to the West to be as vigilant protecting its freedom as she has been to protect her family's. This book is noteworthy for its brevity, its simplicity, and its clear and informed message."
—*Kingston Observer* (MA)

"The gravity of the events Carmen writes of, her insider's perspective, and her engaging style make this memoir a page-turner."
—*Publishers Weekly*

"Saudi Arabia finally comes alive in this story. It is an eye-opening view of a society firmly embedded in the Middle Ages, and seemingly terrified of any change. Carmen Bin Ladin gives us . . . insight into Osama Bin Laden."
—MyShelf.com

INSIDE THE KINGDOM

KINGDOM

My Life in Saudi Arabia

CARMEN BIN LADIN

WARNER BOOKS

NEW YORK   BOSTON

Copyright © 2004 by Carmen Bin Ladin
Postscript © 2005 by Carmen Bin Ladin

Written in collaboration with Ruth Marshall.
All rights reserved.

This work has been previously published in the French, German, Dutch, Italian, and Spanish languages.

Warner Books

Time Warner Book Group
1271 Avenue of the Americas, New York, NY 10020
Visit our Web site at www.twbookmark.com.

Printed in the United States of America

Published in hardcover by Warner Books
First U.S. Trade Edition: June 2005

10 9 8 7 6 5 4 3 2 1

The Library of Congress has catalogued the hardcover edition as follows:

Bin Ladin, Carmen.
    [Voile déchiré. English]
   Inside the kingdom : my life in Saudi Arabia / Carmen Bin Ladin.—1st Warner Books ed.
      p.   cm.
    ISBN 0-446-57708-1
      1. Bin Ladin, Carmen.   2. Women—Saudi Arabia—Biography.
   I. Title: My life in Saudi Arabia.   II. Title.

HQ1730.Z75B5613   2004
305.42'092—dc22

                                                    2004009469

   ISBN: 0-446-69488-6 (pbk.)

Cover design by Flag
Cover photograph by Marie Baldo

This book is dedicated to my daughters
Wafah, Najia, and Noor;
and to my mother.

All the events in this book happened as I described them. However, I have changed the names of two dear friends, Latifa and Turki, at their request, as well as the name of Latifa's father.

Contents

A Letter to My Daughters

My dearest Wafah, Najia, and Noor,

It is with great joy and hope—and also some apprehension—that I undertake the task of writing the story of my life. This book is for you. Of course, you will already have heard some of my stories, and are vaguely aware of the Saudi way of life, but I hope that this will enable you to comprehend the part of your background that you, Wafah and Najia, have completely forgotten and that you, Noor, have never known. Over the years, watching you grow into the beautiful human beings that you are, I came to feel that an insight into my personal experiences of living in Saudi Arabia would also give you a better understanding of the difficult times that you have had to go through since we left the country.

As you know, it is my utmost conviction that freedom of thought and expression is the most valuable gift of all. I want you to never take that freedom for granted. I want to reaffirm what you already know: That although material wealth may give pleasure, it is meaningless when it exists in a golden cage—especially when as a woman you cannot do what you want, or be who you want to be.

Although, for obvious reasons, I have not returned to Saudi Arabia in recent years, I continue to discuss events there with my friends inside the Kingdom. I can see that their lives have not evolved. Deep down in my heart, I am convinced that my decision to raise you with Western values was the right one, even though we have had to sever ties with that country. The only regret that I have—and always will have—is the emotional price that you have paid. I hope it is a consolation to you that I feel honored and privileged to be your mother. Without you I know that I would be a far lesser person: You are the source of my courage, my strength, my will.

Above all I want you to know that any steps that I have taken—whether they were right or wrong—were born out of my love for you. Thank you for what you have given me, by being yourselves. By being you.

CHAPTER 1

9/11

SEPTEMBER 11, 2001, WAS ONE OF THE MOST TRAGIC dates of our lifetimes. It took, and shattered, the lives of thousands of innocent people. It robbed the Western world of its sense of freedom and security. For me, it was a nightmare of grief and horror—one that will imprison me and my three daughters for the rest of our lives.

And yet 9/11 began as a lovely Indian summer day. I was enjoying a leisurely drive from Lausanne to Geneva with my eldest daughter, Wafah, when one of my closest friends, who was working in New York, called me on my cell phone.

"Something terrible just happened," he told me, his voice urgent, from his office in Manhattan. "I'm watching the news. It's incredible: A plane hit one of the towers of the World Trade Center." And then, his voice rising further, he yelled, "Wait a minute—there's another plane—it's going straight toward the second tower. Oh my God"—he was screaming now—"it hit the second tower!"

As he described the second hit, something in me snapped. This was no freak accident. This had to be a deliberately plotted attack, on a country I had always loved and looked on as my second home. I froze. Then waves of horror crashed over me as I realized that somewhere at the bottom of this lay the shadow of my brother-in-law: Osama Bin Laden.*

Beside me in the car, my daughter Wafah was yelling, "What? What happened?" I was in shock. I managed to force out a few words. Wafah lived in New York. She had just graduated from Columbia Law School, and had spent the summer with me in Switzerland. She was planning to head back to her New York apartment in four days' time. Now she was in tears, frantically punching in numbers on her cell phone, trying to reach all her friends.

My first instinct was to call my dearest friend, Mary Martha, in California. I had to hear her voice. She had already heard about the double attack in New York, and she told me a third plane had just hit the Pentagon. The world was spinning off its axis: I could feel it.

I raced to the high school attended by my youngest daughter, Noor. The look of shock in her eyes told me she already knew. The blood had drained from her face.

We rushed home to meet my middle girl, Najia, as she returned from college. She, too, was devastated. Like many millions of other people around the world, the children and I watched CNN, mesmerized, alternately weeping and phoning everyone we knew.

---

*Editor's note: Western transliterations of Arab names vary considerably. In accordance with convention, the spelling "Bin Laden" is used when referring to the clan, and "Bin Ladin" when referring to Yeslam and Carmen.

As the hours passed, my worst fear came true. One man's face and name was on every news bulletin: Osama Bin Laden. My daughters' uncle. A man whose name they shared, but whom they had never met, and whose values were totally foreign to them. I felt a sick sense of doom. This day would change all of our lives, forever.

OSAMA BIN LADEN IS THE YOUNGER BROTHER OF MY husband, Yeslam. He is one of many brothers, and I knew him only distantly, when I lived in Saudi Arabia, years ago. At the time, Osama was a young man, but he always had a commanding presence. Osama was tall, and stern, and his fierce piety was intimidating, even to the more religious members of his family.

During the years that I lived among the Bin Laden family in Saudi Arabia, Osama came to exemplify everything that repelled me in that opaque and harsh country: the unbending dogma that ruled all our lives, the arrogance and pridefulness of the Saudis, and their lack of compassion for people who didn't share their beliefs. That contempt for outsiders, and unyielding orthodoxy, spurred me on to a fourteen-year struggle to give my children a life of freedom.

In my struggle to sever our ties to Saudi Arabia, I began amassing information on my husband's family. I watched as Osama grew in might and notoriety, spiraling deeper into murderous rage against the United States from his redoubt in Afghanistan.

Osama was a warlord, who assisted the Afghan rebels in their fight against the Soviet occupation of their country.

When the Soviets left, Osama returned home, to Saudi Arabia. For many he was already a hero.

When Iraq invaded Kuwait, in 1990, Osama was outraged at the idea that U.S. forces might use Saudi Arabia as a base. He offered Saudi King Fahd the use of his Afghan warriors to fight Saddam Hussein. Some of the more religious princes thought Osama's ideas had merit, but King Fahd refused.

Osama began making incendiary statements against the corruption and moral bankruptcy of the Saudi ruling family, and the Americans who were defending them. Finally, Osama was forced to leave his country, and take refuge in Sudan, where his compound of armed men was surrounded by sentries in tanks. Then he moved back to Afghanistan.

In those days, even though we were separated, I was still on speaking terms with Yeslam, who kept me up-to-date on the evolution in Saudi Arabia and the Bin Laden family news—including Osama's whereabouts. Yeslam told me that Osama's power was growing, despite his exile. Osama, he said, was under the protection of conservative members of the Saudi royal family.

In 1996, when a truck bomb blasted the Khobar Towers living quarters of American forces posted in Dahran, in eastern Saudi Arabia, Osama was mentioned as a possible culprit. I was dumbstruck, yet I knew it could be true. Who else could possibly have at his disposal enough explosives in a country so highly controlled? Osama was a warrior, a zealot, and a member of the family that jointly owned the Bin Laden Organization—the wealthiest and most powerful construction company in Saudi Arabia. I knew of

Osama's fiercely extreme opinions, and deep down I felt that he was capable of a terrible, blind violence.

As attack followed attack, I read everything I could lay my hands on about Osama. So on September 9, 2001, when the news broke of the attack on Afghan fighter Ahmed Shah Massoud, I realized it had to be Osama's doing. I walked over to the television, with a sick feeling. "This is Osama. He is getting ready for something truly awful." "Oh Carmen, you're obsessed," scoffed a friend of mine. But I knew.

I wish I had been wrong.

It never occurred to me that Osama was plotting an assault on the heart of New York. I thought perhaps it would be an embassy—that would have been bad enough. But when the World Trade Center went down in flames just two days after Massoud's death, it hit me again. The sick feeling in my stomach. The fear.

Now I know that it will never go away again.

In the days that followed the attack on the World Trade Center, our lives revolved around the TV news bulletins. The toll of victims kept rising, as the dust settled on the ashen streets of my children's favorite city. We watched people searching for the missing, clutching old snapshots in their hands. Bereaved relatives told reporters about the last phone messages left on their answering machines before their loved ones died. There were those awful photographs of people jumping. I kept thinking, "What if Wafah had been there?" I felt so very deeply for those mothers, for those children.

My three girls were distraught with grief and bewilderment. Noor, the girl who just one year earlier had brought an American flag home from South Carolina to stick on her bedroom wall, sank into despondency. She sobbed, "Mom, New York will never be the same." Fortunately, she never became the target of hostility from her classmates: Her pro-American cheerleading had made her the subject of friendly teasing for years, so all her friends realized how truly hurt my little girl was.

We hardly left the house. Reporters called constantly: I was the only Bin Laden in Europe with a listed phone number. Friends called, their voices strained. Then they stopped calling. We were rapidly becoming personae non grata. The Bin Laden name frightened even the hardiest professionals. A new law firm refused to take my divorce case: I suddenly found myself without a lawyer.

Of all of us, it was Najia who focused most on the suffering of the World Trade Center's victims. She couldn't bear to watch TV most of the time. Her name was becoming public currency: This was particularly hard to bear for such a private person. Najia is perhaps the most discreet of all my children. She doesn't display her emotions easily, but I could see she was stricken.

The terrible irony was that we identified, and grieved, with the victims, while the outside world saw us as aggressors. We were trapped in a Kafkaesque situation—particularly Wafah. After four years of law school, Wafah's life was in New York. Her apartment was just blocks from the World Trade Center. She talked night and day about her friends there; she felt she had to be in New York, and wanted to fly back immediately.

Then one newspaper reported that Wafah had been

tipped off: She had, they said, fled New York just days before the attack. This was untrue. Wafah had been with me, in Switzerland, since June. But other papers picked up the story. They said Wafah had known in advance about the attack, and had done nothing to protect the people and the home that she loved.

A friend who was staying in Wafah's New York apartment called: She had begun receiving death threats. It was an understandable reaction—how could strangers distinguish one Bin Laden from another?

I felt I had no choice. I alone could defend my daughters. I issued a statement saying that my three girls and I had had no connection whatsoever with this evil, barbaric attack on America, a country we loved and whose values we shared and admired. I went on TV. I wrote to the newspapers to express our sorrow. My long battle to free myself and my children from the ideals of Saudi Arabia was all the evidence I could offer for our innocence: that, and our goodwill, and the pain we felt for Osama's victims.

I had so longed for an end to my bitter fight against the Bin Ladens and their country. But now I faced a whole new struggle. I would have to shepherd my children through the anguish they felt as their name became synonymous with evil, infamy, and death.

My private life had become a public story.

IRONICALLY, IT WAS ONLY AFTER SEPTEMBER 11 THAT my fourteen-year fight for freedom from Saudi Arabia made sense to the people around me. Before that, I think no one truly understood what was at stake—not the courts, not the judge, not even my friends. Even in my own country, Switzerland, I was perceived, more or less, as just another woman embroiled in a nasty international divorce.

But I always knew that my fight went far deeper than that. I was fighting to gain freedom from one of the most powerful societies and families in the world—to salvage my daughters from a merciless culture that denied their most basic rights. In Saudi Arabia they could not even walk alone in the street, let alone choose the path of their own lives. I fought to free them from the hard-core fundamentalist values of Saudi Arabian society, and its contempt for the tolerance and liberty of the West, which I have learned to value deeply.

I am afraid that even today, the West does not fully understand Saudi Arabia and its rigid value system. For nine years, I lived inside the powerful Bin Laden clan, with its close and complex links to the royal family. My daughters went to Saudi schools. I lived, to a great extent, the life of a Saudi woman. And over time, I learned and analyzed the mechanisms of that opaque society, and the harsh and bitter rules that it enforces on its daughters.

I could not stand quietly by while my little girls' bright minds were extinguished. I could not teach them to submit to the values of Saudi Arabia. I could not watch them be branded as rebels because of the Western values that I taught them—despite all the punishment that might ensue. And were they to comply with Saudi society, I could not face the prospect that my daughters might grow up to become like the faceless, voiceless women I lived among.

Above all I could not watch my daughters be denied what I valued most: freedom of choice. I had to free them, and myself.

This is my story.

CHAPTER 2

A Secret Garden

THERE WAS A CAREFREE FEELING IN THE AIR THE year I met my husband, Yeslam. It was 1973, and young people ruled the world. I was outgoing and sociable, a couple of years out of high school. But I felt a little lost that summer, as I looked around me for the path I wanted my life to take. I was interested in the law; I wanted to defend the defenseless. I wanted to travel, and have adventures; I wanted to give my life a sense of meaning. But my mother, who came from an aristocratic Persian family, was bent on my getting safely married.

My three sisters and I would often crowd into one of our bedrooms, in my mother's house outside Geneva, and listen to Beatles LPs, talking about our future. I was the eldest, and I suppose I talked the most. I always insisted, in those days, that I would never marry a Middle Easterner, as my mother would have liked. I was attracted to the freer lives of the Americans I had seen as a little girl at the American Club near my great-aunt's house in Iran. Their lives seemed brave, modern—free. They drove jeeps, wore jeans, ate hamburgers, whereas people from the Middle East lived lives that seemed so closed off, hobbled by layers of tradition and secrecy, where appearances seemed more important than desires.

I was Swiss—born in Lausanne, to a Swiss father and a Persian mother. My mother's family, the Sheibanys, was cultivated and aristocratic. When I was little, my mother took us to Iran for long vacations every year or so. I loved Iran—the spicy food, so subtle and aromatic; what seemed like acres of roses tended by invisible gardeners in my grandmother's high-walled garden; and the grand old house where my mother had grown up, with its blue-tiled steam room dim with vapor, the huge library of ancient books, the latticework shutters, the richly colored carpets and fine antiques.

When I was a child, I thought Iran was a special country—high in color and drama. I loved the months we spent there. My grandmother treated me like a little princess. I adored her, and I knew she adored me.

One time when I was seven or eight, my mother gave a party in my grandmother's house in Iran. The rooms were filled with the people she had grown up with: well-known writers and intellectuals from old families, who shared my grandmother's aristocratic scorn for the parvenu Shah. Their discussions were way above my head, but the atmosphere was exciting. When the time came to go to bed, I refused point-blank to go upstairs to my room.

"Daddy is coming," I kept insisting—though my mother told me again and again that he was in Switzerland, hard at work. I wore my mother's patience to shreds that night.

Then just as I was about to give up and go to bed, my beloved father walked through the door. He hadn't phoned ahead: He had just impulsively taken an airplane. I was overjoyed and, wickedly, triumphant.

When my grandmother realized that there truly was no way I could possibly have known in advance of my father's arrival, she bent over and held me at arm's length as she looked in my eyes: "Carmen," she said, "you are a very special person. Never forget that."

Every child should feel the way I felt that night.

My grandmother had a swimming pool, and my handsome, charming Swiss father used to dive straight into it from the upper floor, to our squeals of horror and delight. One day my little sister Béatrice, a toddler, fell in, and my mother, decked out in an elaborate pink silk dress with a tight waist and wide skirt, leapt into the pool to save her. Her skirt puffed out hugely, like a parachute. To this day I can see my mother emerging with my little sister in her arms, fully clothed, water streaming from her dress, but nonetheless still beautiful.

I was a curious child, and like many children I could sense the importance of adult conversations, even when the details were beyond my understanding. I loved to listen in to political discussions. As far back as I can remember, all my life I have sought to analyze things around me, even when they seem far beyond my reach.

When I was about seven, my grandmother's household went into terrible turmoil when a cousin of my mother's, Abbas, was arrested and tortured by the Shah's fearsome

SAVAK secret police. They claimed he was a member of the Communist Tudeh Party.

That summer, the big song on the radio was "Marabebous"—a song about a man who is sentenced to death, asking his daughter to kiss him for the last time. I used to play that song again and again, full of sorrow. I wanted to know why that man had to die. I wondered if my mother's cousin would have to die, too. What had he done? I suppose this was the first time I realized that someone could pay for their beliefs with their life.

Iran was my secret garden, something that made me different from the other little Swiss girls in our local school outside Lausanne. But when I was nine, my mother suddenly cut off all connection with Iran. My father had left her, and she didn't want to admit it. If she acknowledged that her marriage had failed, she would lose face with her relatives. So, rather than tell the truth, she withdrew from any close contact with her own family.

For a long time my mother didn't even tell us, her four daughters, that she and my father were separating. She told us he was away, on business, but my instinct told me otherwise. I knew that this was the way my mother lived: If something was disagreeable, you evaded it, denied it, suppressed it. If you never spoke of it, it didn't exist. What counted was saving face.

After my father left our family, my mother brought us up alone, with the help of a governess. For years, I had no contact with my father at all, and nobody explained why. I learned not to ask. I realized early on that I must live between two cultures, caught somewhere between the Iran that had shaped my mother's strict rules of behavior, and the local Swiss school I attended. Home was a strange, silent space where everything important was unspoken.

I knew that my mother was born a Muslim, because her father had been one—in Islam, you take your father's beliefs. But my mother wore her Islam lightly. She didn't practice it in any formal sense. I saw her pray a handful of times, but not in the traditional sense of bowing and kneeling, facing Mecca. If she wanted to pray, she might just as easily enter a church as a mosque. She didn't fast during the Ramadan month, or wear a headscarf. I saw my grandmother veiled occasionally, when she had sheep killed and distributed as alms to the poor. Being a Muslim seemed natural if you were from the Middle East. But it didn't enforce any regimented lifestyle on my mother or on us children.

It was my mother's sense of propriety that restricted our lives as normal Swiss girls. There was no rough play or rumpled clothes, no late-night parties or dates. (Like all teenagers, we learned to circumvent those strict rules: We weren't angels, and she never locked us in.) Although it was important to her that we continue our studies, marriage was her ultimate goal for us.

My mother tried to direct every detail of our lives. Until I was older, and openly rebelled, our mother dressed the four of us exactly alike, down to the ribbons in our plaits. "You can be perfectly elegant, but if you have a single stain you are nothing," she would say. For my mother, decorum was vital.

When I was an adult one of my mother's cousins told

me the story of my parents' marriage. My mother had come
to Lausanne to study, and met my father. They eloped to
Paris, and when they came back they were married: There
was nothing her family could do about it. This was the kind
of person she was, underneath—impetuous and rebellious,
the kind of woman who would name her daughters Carmen, Salomé, Béatrice, and Magnolia. My mother left her
country, eloped with the man of her choice, drove a car. In
a way, strangely, my mother was a pioneer.

But later she suppressed that personality—maybe because her marriage had failed. As we grew up, my mother
seemed to care only about what other people would think.
She insisted on bringing up her children within the bounds
of conventions that she herself had sought to flee. She
couldn't admit that my father had left her for someone
else, because if her marriage had failed, that would prove to
her own mother that her elopement had been wrong.

That was what it meant to me, to be from the Middle
East. You lived behind secrets. You hid things that were
disagreeable. You had to submit to the conventions of society. Saving face could justify dishonesty. Only appearance mattered.

My personality was different. To me, truth was important. And I didn't like to submit. Instead of bending to my
mother's rules, I began confronting her, defiantly. I remember telling her to stop pushing me into situations where I
would have to lie to her. I wanted to force her to accept the
reality of my character.

In high school, both my sister Salomé and I started to
smoke. My mother offered to buy us anything we wanted if

we gave up our cigarettes. Salomé wanted a car, so my mother bought her a Fiat, but Salomé kept on smoking, in secret.

My mother took me to a furrier's, had me try on a leopard-skin coat. She told me, "Promise me now you will never smoke another cigarette. I will buy it, right now, to-day." I wanted to—I wanted that coat—but I didn't want to make a promise that I knew I could not keep.

As I grew into adulthood, I found myself in moral turmoil, handicapped by the contradictions in my upbringing and personality. I lived in the West. I was impetuous, impulsive—I longed to be free. But so much of my background lay in the conventions of Middle Eastern culture, where clan rules are more important than personality. In the Middle East, you never develop as an individual. People may manage to escape their traditions for a short while, but then those rules catch up to them.

I knew I should decide for myself what path my life should take. But I was too inexperienced and mixed-up to do it alone. I was waiting for help—for some sort of sign.

CHAPTER 3

Falling in Love

T HE FIRST TIME I MET YESLAM, I HAD NO IDEA THAT
this man would change my life forever. It was the spring,
and Geneva was full of Saudi Arabian tourists. My sisters
and I were planning a vacation to visit my grandmother in
Iran, so my mother had agreed to rent out one floor of her
house for the summer to a Saudi Arabian family vacation-
ing in Europe. This slight young Saudi man, dressed in
black from head to toe, had come to finalize the agreement. I glanced at him; he smiled politely.

Then my grandmother injured her leg, and our trip to
Iran was canceled. It was too late to call off the rental. So my
sisters and I shuttled between an apartment in Lausanne
and my mother's house, where she hosted her Saudi guests.

Yeslam's mother was Iranian, like mine: a soft-spoken
woman, with a sweet, round face and darkly dyed hair. She
wore long dresses and a simple Muslim head covering. We
spoke in Persian. Yeslam's younger brothers Ibrahim and
Khalil had wild Afros and platform shoes. Fawzia, the
younger sister, looked like any European teenager, with tight

T-shirts, long wavy hair, and big tinted sunglasses. And then there was Yeslam.

Yeslam intrigued me. He was calm, but he had a compelling authority. He was slim, bronzed, handsome. He didn't speak much, but his eyes were penetrating, and gentle. And mostly they looked at me.

Slowly, we began talking in English together; simple chitchat evolved into long conversations. As time passed, Yeslam became increasingly attentive. He began insisting that I accompany him and his family on their trips around town. Yeslam was crazy about his two Dobermans. He was twenty-four years old, a little older than my friends and I, and different. Yeslam acted like a grown-up. He did as he pleased. He was responsible, and leadership seemed to come naturally to him. For everybody—even his mother, his brothers and sisters—Yeslam's word was law. Even my mother started to look to him for direction.

I can see now that Yeslam's natural authority came from the Saudi culture in which he grew up, where the oldest son commands every gesture of his clan. Then, though, I saw only a man who was courting me, who was exotic and beautiful, and whose company I came to find fascinating.

Yeslam was calm and clear-sighted. He had a sharp mind and a strong will. And he remembered every detail of anything I said. He understood me. He seemed to need me and I began to feel that I was the only person in the world in whom he could confide. There was no moment when I could say that I suddenly fell for him. But I had fallen in love.

As the summer passed, Yeslam and I began to look for each other every day. We spent every free moment together.

I had just found my parents' divorce papers, and reading the whole story devastated me. I saw my father in a different light. The handsome, commanding, adoring Daddy whom I had longed for was small, petty, mean. My mother, it seemed, had hidden so many things from me—important things, which I felt I deserved to know.

I cried on Yeslam's shoulder, and told him I could never get married, because I never wanted my children to be abandoned by their father, as my father had abandoned my sisters and me. I never wanted them to suffer through a bitter divorce, like my parents'. Yeslam gave me comfort. I felt that he understood me. With Yeslam, I felt safe.

Yeslam had an elegant way about him. One night he tried to teach me to drive in his Porsche; I smashed it into my mother's gateway. I thought he'd be upset, but he didn't seem to really mind; he just smiled. "You're a dangerous driver," he told me. Yeslam liked his brand-new car, but that night I realized he liked me even more.

Driving was one of Yeslam's passions. He had taken lessons in racecar driving in Sweden. We spent afternoons together speeding across the Swiss mountains, blaring Schubert on the car stereo.

In the beginning of our love affair I saw Yeslam only as a boyfriend, not as a prospective suitor. One of the things that most attracted me to him was that he seemed so independent—and I wanted so much to be independent, too. I loved to talk with him. When he sulked it drove me crazy. He never told me off, but if I spent too much time talking with my friends he would go quiet, and instantly I felt guilty. He wanted all my attention, all the time. He was so reserved with everyone except for me. He loved that I was outgoing, but I didn't want to make him uncomfortable—I understood that there were limits. Strangely, his possessiveness flattered me. It felt reassuring.

Our affair was becoming more than just a summer romance. Yeslam began involving me in his private life, introducing me to his extended family. He told me that he had twenty-four brothers and twenty-nine sisters. I couldn't even begin to imagine what that really meant in practical terms, and I suppose my shock showed on my face, because Yeslam assured me this was an unusually large family, even by Saudi Arabian standards.

I met Yeslam's oldest brother, Salem, when he passed through Switzerland. I was impressed by how open and gregarious he was compared to Yeslam. Salem had a great sense of fun—he laughed a lot, and played "Oh! Susannah" on the harmonica. He seemed very Westernized in comparison to Yeslam, who was so discreet. But I could also see there was a complex power struggle underlying their relationship.

Though he couldn't have been more than thirty years old, Salem had an almost paternal attitude toward Yeslam, and Yeslam resented it. "Salem thinks that just because he's the head of the family, he's in charge of me," he told me, with barely restrained annoyance. "But I don't need Salem's permission to do anything." It seemed we shared a struggle—me with my mother; Yeslam with his brother.

One afternoon, as the summer ended, we were walking with Yeslam's dogs in my mother's garden and began talking about the future. Yeslam said he wanted to return to Saudi Arabia and breed Dobermans. I thought that was ludicrous. I saw great potential in Yeslam; I felt he was exceptional. I told him he was too intelligent to be content with that—he owed it to himself to have more ambition. He must keep studying, and make something of his life. Yeslam said, "I will, but only if you marry me." It was like a challenge, a kind of dare. And in a way, I heard it as an appeal. Yeslam, too, was waiting for someone to show him his path. So I knew it wasn't a joke—he meant it.

I laughed, and said I'd think about it. But we both knew that I meant yes.

Yeslam stayed on at my mother's house after the summer ended. He was my fiancé now, which meant I was a grown-up, which meant I was free. There was a man in the family, as there hadn't been for many years, and my mother loved that. I think in a way she felt that her rebellious daughter was someone else's responsibility now. She no longer questioned me about where I was going when I went out, or demanded I return at fixed hours.

We went out to nightclubs, like any young couple in Switzerland. Yeslam was a good dancer, but not as exuberant as Salem. Yeslam told me pointedly that I shouldn't dance with Salem if he asked me to. If I did, then Salem might get the wrong impression of me. This was one of my first introductions to the many odd rules of Saudi Arabia. If you dance with another man—even your boyfriend's brother—you're not respected.

Our first disagreement took place in the Lausanne train

station. I wanted something to eat, and there was a long line of people waiting to buy sandwiches. Yeslam went straight up to the sandwich vendor; the man rather rudely ordered him to take his place in the line. Yeslam did something unexpected: He threw down a 100 Swiss franc note on the counter and walked off. That Yeslam had marched to the front of the queue was one thing—perhaps he hadn't understood that other people were waiting to be served. But to throw down a large amount of money and walk off? It was so strange.

Later, I told him I didn't understand his reaction—that to me it seemed as though he had rewarded the man for his rudeness. But Yeslam couldn't tolerate being told what to do by a stranger. He didn't submit, and go back to queue up; he didn't rage at the man, either. He threw money at him, to show his scorn. To Yeslam, this was logical. For the first time, though, I found his behavior puzzling.

Yeslam and I became formally engaged in October. My mother now felt certain that I would marry Yeslam; that gave her peace of mind, and brought me freedom. In November, Yeslam took me to Lebanon, the birthplace of one of my favorite philosophers, Kahlil Gibran. (His book *The Prophet* had been my constant companion as a teenager.) It was glorious, like a fairy tale.

I was a grown-up woman traveling with a man who loved me. To me, Lebanon was part of the Arab world, a civilization that had been the home of visionary and wise men who had discovered the secrets of the stars, and mathematics. Beirut before the civil war was like the Arabia of the *Thousand and*

One Nights: the opulence, the colors, the smells, and above all, the orange-yellow sunlight of the Mediterranean. Yeslam was endlessly attentive. We stayed up late and ate what we liked, did what we wanted. It was wonderful to be in love. It gave me a new perspective on my life.

It seemed like everywhere we went we encountered more of Yeslam's brothers. In Lebanon we met Ali and Tabet. Physically they were very different. Ali was tall, very Middle Eastern–looking: His mother was Lebanese. Tabet's mother was Ethiopian: He was black. It was only then that I realized that Yeslam's father had had twenty-two wives. Rather than let the implications sink in, I chose to see it as an exotic backdrop. I was in love, and this labyrinth of family ties was all just another hazy part of my wonderful romance.

We went on to Iran, where we spent three days with some of my mother's relatives (though not my grandmother—she was in the United States for medical reasons). There, the blindfold fell from my eyes. As a child, on vacations, I had seen beggars in the street: They came often to my grandmother's neighborhood, for handouts of food or old clothes. One of my uncles would always dismiss our pity: "Oh, don't fret so—they have money, they just don't want to work."

When Yeslam took me to the carpet bazaar in Tehran to buy a Persian carpet, I saw terrible misery. Small boys and old men were doubled over under bales of carpets. They should have been in school, or at home—they seemed far too fragile to be working. Instead they were laden like donkeys. My life had been so sheltered. I had never seen such a thing. I started crying.

Yeslam took me back to the car. Our driver tried to console me. He said, "You think those people are poor? They're lucky—they have work. I can take you to where families live in holes dug out of the earth." It made it worse: I was inconsolable. Even Yeslam couldn't comfort me. I realized that the Iran I recalled from childhood had been an illusion, disguising a harsh reality that I had never even seen. Everything that had seemed certain was based on secrets and mirages.

Later, when I imagined that Saudi Arabia would resemble my childhood memories of Iran, I would be fooling myself twice over.

I was still hesitant about marrying Yeslam. I was young; and the bitter example of my parents was still vivid for me. Marriage was scary. But we had told my mother of our plans. The machine had begun rolling, and it was carrying me with it.

In December 1973 we flew to the United States together, to register for college. America was thrilling. It was my childhood dream come true. People really did live lives that were carefree and easygoing. They seemed so much less tied down by convention than anyone I had ever known. I loved the huge spaces, the way of life, the sense of freedom—the incredible sense of stepping into the future.

America truly seemed to be the land of opportunity, and not just for studying. It was clear to Yeslam and to me that this incredibly open country offered us business opportunities, too. On our first visit to look at the campus of the University of Southern California, in Los Angeles, we met Jerry Vulk, the director of international students. (He told us later he'd spotted us as foreigners immediately. My skirt and high heels, and Yeslam's European suit, made us stand out a mile away.) Jerry took us under his wing, and showed us around. We decided to start classes right away, in the month of January. Yeslam would be studying business; I would have to take remedial English.

Then we flew back to Geneva, for our first Christmas together, with my family. Yeslam seemed perfectly happy. He didn't seem at all shocked that although my mother was Iranian, and Muslim, my family had a Christmas tree and exchanged presents—that we celebrated a Christian holiday.

A couple of weeks after our first semester began, we met Jerry's wife, Mary Martha Barkley. It was her birthday—later on, she always called us her birthday gift. Sometimes in life you meet someone you connect with immediately; for me, Mary Martha was like that. She was a real lady, tall, with dark hair and blue eyes—a great beauty. The more I saw of Mary Martha, the more I liked her. She had a wonderful way of carrying herself, a sense of style, and great warmth. She was kind. Mary Martha helped Yeslam and me find a house to rent—the first in a long series of thoughtful, gracious gestures.

Mary Martha became my role model, my ideal American. Her example helped me resolve the loose ends of my personality—helped me to become the adult I aspired to be. Watching Mary Martha, I felt bits of the puzzle of my upbringing falling into place. I loved her nature: independent but tender, optimistic and funny, elegant and direct in her speech. I admired the way she related to her teenaged children and taught them to grow strong and true. Mary Martha was an utterly devoted mother—she woke at four every morning to take her son to swimming practice—and yet she never seemed to pressure her children to act against their will.

This was the way I would bring up my own children, I thought: to be themselves. Mary Martha never judged me, or sought to direct my life as my mother did. She and I became more than friends; we developed a deep and enduring bond. I admired her more than anyone in the world, and she never disappointed me. She was like a mother to me over the years to come—my American mom.

One of the students in my English class was a Saudi named Abdelatif. He was dumbstruck when he heard I was engaged to Yeslam Bin Ladin. He came up to me one day, very formally, to say that he had known Yeslam's father, who had died in 1967. On the other side of the world, Abdelatif was the first person to open my eyes to the body of Saudi legends surrounding Sheikh Mohamed Bin Laden. His own father had worked for Sheikh Mohamed in Jeddah, Abdelatif said: Indeed, almost everyone in Jeddah did. Yeslam's father had been born with nothing, and had built one of the most powerful construction companies in the Middle East, Abdelatif told me. Sheikh Mohamed had built the palaces of kings and princes, and renovated the holiest sites of Islam. He was a giant among men; a hero, who worked harder than anyone on earth. He was honest, pious, beloved by everyone who met him. And I was in love with his son.

We invited Abdelatif and his wife for dinner. Later, she taught me to cook Saudi food. (I still make those recipes—sambousas, minced meat in pastry, remains one of my children's favorites—but I was an inexperienced cook. We ate a lot of takeout that year.) Abdelatif's wife was young, but she dressed modestly, like an old lady, in drab long skirts. A headscarf was always tightly clamped around her face. She was very reserved. Abdelatif was always rather shy with me, too, especially in class, when Yeslam wasn't around. He never seemed to look me in the eye.

I thought then that it was because of the Bin Laden connection. It was only much later that I realized that he was not permitted to look at the face of a woman who belonged to another Saudi man.

But Saudi Arabia was far away in those carefree days. Yeslam had left the country young—he was just six when Sheikh Mohamed sent him to boarding school in Lebanon, and later to England and Sweden, and he had spent only summers at home after that. I had no plans to live in faraway Saudi Arabia. And we were so happy in America. I felt that Yeslam was building our future in this wonderful, free new country that we were discovering. America was our home now.

And if one day Yeslam's destiny took him to Saudi Arabia, so be it. We would be pioneers. At last I had found my mission in life. Sheikh Mohamed, Yeslam's father, had taken the kingdom of Saudi Arabia from sandy camel paths to high-rises and airports. Yeslam, with my help, could encourage it to grow further, to become a modern society.

In those days, I had no fear and felt no limits. I had found my life's partner and I felt I could take on the world. My temerity knew no bounds. I knew nothing.

CHAPTER 4

My Saudi Wedding

I HAD A LITTLE STONE THAT I'D PICKED UP FROM MY great-aunt's grave in Iran. It lay on my dressing table, set with a bit of silver on a chain. It was just a piece of gravel really, but I treasured it. The day I'd picked it up, standing by that grave with Yeslam, I'd felt in need of guidance. It was as if I asked my great-aunt a question—should I marry this man? The stone had come to stand as a kind of symbol of my relationship with Yeslam. Now, I realized one April morning in our Los Angeles house, I couldn't find my little stone.

"That's it!" I announced to Yeslam. "It means we can't get married."

Yeslam took it so seriously. He could be so disarming. He hunted everywhere—he even emptied the garbage—and then triumphantly discovered my precious stone in the back of my dresser. "Now you have to marry me," he crowed.

That's when I realized how much I meant to Yeslam. He deeply wanted me to marry him.

My mother kept pressuring us to give her a date for our

wedding. She liked Yeslam; I think she felt confident that he could temper my impetuous character. And she was so eager to have a man in the family again. So Yeslam and I finally decided that when the semester ended, I would return to Geneva while Yeslam went to Saudi Arabia, to make arrangements for us to be married before the summer ended. Saudis may marry foreigners only if the King gives his authorization, and Yeslam needed to go there to get his permission.

I wanted us to get married in Geneva, among all my family and friends: After all, the Bin Ladens had the means to make such a trip. But when Yeslam returned with the King's permission, he told me he wanted us to marry in Jeddah, his family home. He said that would prove to all that the King had officially agreed that Yeslam could marry me, a foreigner. Yeslam said that people might not respect me as much if we married abroad. Again, there was the peculiar need to earn respect, and the strange, almost feudal rituals with which I would have to earn it. It amazed me that the King's official permission would make me more worthy of respect. It seemed funny, not threatening.

Preparations were already underway for the wedding of one of his sisters, Regaih, Yeslam told me. It would be easiest if ours was scheduled for the same day—August 8, 1974. I couldn't begin to imagine what a Saudi wedding would be like. I had never even been to the country. I didn't question it. I was in love; my mother was delighted that I was getting married. For me this wedding was increasingly becoming just a formality.

I brought no friends: Getting visas for me and my family

was ordeal enough. There was only my mother, my sisters, and Mamal, the son of my great-aunt, who came from Iran.

I chose not to ask my father to come—I didn't want my mother to have to confront him after all those years. I felt my mother still loved him, and that seeing him would cause her too much pain. So Mamal, my mother's cousin, was my closest male relative, although I didn't know him well, and it seemed as though his presence was almost as important as my own. Mamal would participate in the men-only religious ceremony, where he would represent the bride, and take Yeslam's hand. His presence would certify that Yeslam and I could be married. Without Mamal, it seemed, there could be no wedding.

It seemed like such a droll concept. Whenever she caught sight of Mamal, my sister Magnolia used to joke, "Look, here comes the bride!"

My preparations were hurried. First I went out to buy a wedding dress. I looked at the haute couture at Chanel in Geneva, but none of the models were anything like the dress I wanted—or suitable for what I imagined of Saudi Arabia, based on my childhood memories of Iran. I wanted a high collar, scalloped sleeves with a cuff, something completely simple and yet perfectly elegant. In the end I designed a dress that was made up by a Chanel tailor in white organza. I felt it was truly me.

Next came the veils. A long wedding veil in white organza; and the black cloak that would shield my face and body from the world around me in Yeslam's country. Yeslam had explained that I would need one.

I bought the thick black cotton and had it made up. The

result was a heavy Persian veil, like a chador, not the thinner, silk Saudi abaya. I didn't know any better. The thing was like a curtain, covering me from head to toe, so heavy it almost stood up on its own. It seemed almost comically antiquated, like wearing a disguise.

Last, my sisters and I went out shopping for the many long dresses that Yeslam had told me we would need. But in all of Geneva we could find nothing even remotely appropriate: dresses that were formal, yet modest, for parties; simpler, day dresses that were not too casual, yet long. We had to have a tailor make up a whole series of garments. Finally, my sisters had salmon-pink bridesmaids' dresses made, too. We were all caught up in a flurry of fittings.

Then Yeslam and I took the plane to Jeddah, with my sister Salomé. (My mother and my other two sisters followed us two days later.) Yeslam wore the white cotton Saudi robe called a thobe. It is quite crisp and elegant when it is done well: I thought him even more romantic in this exotic costume. A few minutes before we landed, Salomé and I put on our veils. We were covered completely in thick black cloth—hands, head, body. Just our feet stuck out. Even our eyes were hidden behind the impenetrable black gauze. I looked over at Salomé. It was a shock. She had no face.

I watched the desert approach as we landed. The light through the black gauze cloth was so dim, I didn't know if this new country was simply the darkest, emptiest place I had ever seen, or if the cloth across my eyes was preventing me from seeing anything that was there. It gave me a strange, oppressive feeling. This was not like when I had tried the veil on at the tailor's in Geneva. Then I had been excited—I was getting married—but now I felt a sense of melancholy inside me, an apprehension that met the blackness of the outside world.

The heat was stifling. I could hardly breathe under the thick folds of my abaya. Every movement was slow and awkward. We came down the steps of the plane, and my sister stumbled on the stairs. Everything spilled out of her beauty case, and yet nobody helped her up or picked up anything. She turned to me, a completely black triangle speaking, and said, "What is this place?" In Saudi Arabia, no man could touch her, or even come too close.

I was so fixated on keeping the veil in place, I couldn't pay attention to anything else. I caught sight of Yeslam's brother Ibrahim, with his crinkly eyes and friendly face. I loudly called, "Hi, Ibrahim"—I was so relieved, to see someone familiar—but he said nothing. He looked almost embarrassed. Then, very softly, he said "Hi." I had forgotten, although Yeslam had warned me: I was not permitted to speak to any man in public.

Just a few minutes in Saudi Arabia, and I had already made my first blunder. It was beginning to dawn on me that in Yeslam's country I was going to have to keep quiet in public.

We drove off, not even waiting for our suitcases. Some nameless underling would take care of that now. I looked out of the car window and through my veil I saw just a dim light—no people, no buildings. Even the streetlights were dark.

In fact, there was very little to see. Jeddah at the time

was just a small town, dingy and old, and the neighborhood where most of the Bin Ladens lived together was on the road out toward Mecca, at the very edge of the desert.

The road went bumpy, then smooth, and suddenly we were at Yeslam's home—Kilometer Seven on the Mecca Road. The gate was open, and my mother-in-law was standing in the threshold of the house.

We always called my mother-in-law Om Yeslam. She had a name of her own, of course, but it was never used. Like most women in the Kingdom, she took the name of her eldest son. (If she has only daughters, a Saudi woman carries the name of her firstborn—until a son comes, and his name supersedes his sister's.)

Om Yeslam was pleasant and welcoming. It was a relief to be able to take off my abaya. Suddenly the light inside the house seemed blinding. There were so many chandeliers blazing, it was like stepping into a lamp shop. We sat down, and made small talk. After the first greetings, I began to take in my new surroundings. Everything inside the house seemed to be green. Dark green wall-to-wall carpeting, green wallpaper, green-gold velvet sofas arranged around the four walls of the sitting room. It was really quite odd-looking. There were plastic flowers, too. When I went to wash up, I discovered my bedroom had a dark maroon marble bathroom, like a tomb, with no windows. There were no rich old carpets or fine antique workmanship: The house was new, and awkward, like a raw suburban tract home.

The servants came in with the evening meal. They spread a cloth on the floor and we ate there: lebna cheese, honey, cucumber salad, flat bread, yogurt, bean paste. The lack of sophistication surprised me. I had imagined an exotic Oriental abode, like in the movies, or like my grandmother's home in Iran. After all, Yeslam's father had been one of the richest men in Saudi Arabia. But this was just a basic house, furnished in poor taste, where people lived very simply. It was not at all the life of refinement and elegance I had imagined.

My mother-in-law was a soft-spoken and amiable woman—never harsh with me, although I know she must have been disappointed that her son had not chosen to marry a Saudi. We chatted. Our conversation was stilted, in Farsi and English, interspersed with Yeslam's translations into Arabic.

The next day the round of visitors commenced. Since I was a bride-to-be, the family had to come to congratulate me—and, more importantly, to examine me. I faced an endless stream of women—only women—all in formal, long dresses—laden down with lots of jewelry. There were dozens of them. They had unfamiliar names that I found difficult to retain. It was a blur.

Most of those visitors were Yeslam's relatives. The abstract idea—twenty-two wives, twenty-five sons, twenty-nine daughters—was beginning to take form before my eyes. It was bewildering.

Salem, whom I had already met in Geneva, was the oldest son. Yeslam was the tenth in line. Nobody told me the order of birth of the sisters, as they flowed through the door. It manifestly didn't matter, and I didn't even think to ask.

Of course Yeslam's father, Sheikh Mohamed, hadn't been married to all his wives at the same time. He divorced some as he married others. Most of the wives, divorced or current, as well as their children, had lived inside the patriarch's huge compound in Jeddah while Yeslam was growing up.

But just before Sheikh Mohamed died, he had begun building a number of new houses, seven kilometers along the Mecca Road out of town. Many of his children moved there after his death, and took their mothers along with them. It was a whole Bin Laden neighborhood of separate houses, laid out along three streets that were isolated at the edge of the desert.

We lived those first days in Kilometer Seven in almost hypnotic inactivity. There was nothing to do except welcome an endless rustling of female visitors in formal clothes and drink cardamom-spiced Arabic coffee in tiny cups. At first, I didn't know I should shake my cup to signify that I had had enough, and didn't want to be served anymore. I've never drunk so much coffee in my life! Finally, when I explained my problem, Om Yeslam kindly explained.

Only the men could come and go as they pleased. We women were confined to the house—not only because of the sweltering summer heat, but because we could not be seen unveiled by men outside the family.

Even to go into the garden we had to notify the male employees to vacate the premises. Once the coast was clear, we would step out, usually at dusk, into a furnace. The sand of the desert around us was blinding—like staring at Alpine snow without sunglasses. In this way my freewheeling universe had shrunk to one and a half acres of baking garden planted with a few spindly trees.

We took no exercise. Walking anywhere was completely unthinkable. There was, in any case, nowhere we could go. No hotels, sports arenas, theaters, swimming pools, restaurants—if they existed at all, they were only for men. No ice cream parlors, parks, or shops: A woman of quality could almost never shop. No male other than Yeslam could see my face. True, Yeslam had warned me about all this before I'd arrived. But living it was very different. It was unreal.

Om Yeslam's life was entirely sealed off from any men, apart from her relatives. Her Ethiopian driver never saw her unveiled. I'm not sure if he ever even heard her voice. Her young houseboy—he was about twelve, and also Ethiopian— would take her orders and instruct the driver when to be ready and where to go.

I remember the look of astonishment and dismay that passed between my mother-in-law and Yeslam's sister Fawzia when I first thanked their maid—just for something trivial, like a cup of tea. It was quite startling. And I remember the surprise, and a kind of joy, that sprang into that young woman's face.

My mother's family had plenty of servants in Iran, as a matter of course, and even in Switzerland we had a governess. But this was another world, and there was something unpleasant about it.

Later I was to visit many houses, and surprise many women by thanking their servants. This contempt for the staff highlighted the fact that Saudi Arabia was one of the last countries in the world to outlaw slavery. Until 1962, it was still common for grand families to own slaves. The government finally bought their freedom. Twelve years later, when I arrived in Saudi Arabia, servants were still largely not considered autonomous human beings worthy of thanks.

Every gesture in this strange new world seemed foreign. The people around me were inscrutable. Men could not look at me, even veiled. The family was friendly, but I could read nothing in their eyes. It was almost ethereal, this monotonous denial. I felt hypnotized. It was nothing like Iran or Beirut—it was another planet. There were so many things to absorb at once, and I didn't know what to think of them.

I discovered the city of Jeddah in daylight when we went to the Swiss embassy to register our imminent marriage, after three days in the country. (If I did not record that I wished to retain my nationality prior to the wedding I would lose my Swiss passport. Later, I was to bless that day many times.) It was my first release from the house. The air was so hot I could hardly breathe under the thick veil. Yeslam had to remind me that I must sit in the back of the car, completely covered, while he drove.

Driving through Jeddah, staring from behind the tinted windows of the Mercedes, I watched a roadside scene from another millennium. Saudi Arabia was still emerging in those days from the crushing poverty of its traditional way of life. People had become a little less poor after oil was discovered in the 1930s, but the crazy bonanza of wealth that would sweep over the country after the 1973 oil embargo lay in the future. Donkey Square was a crisscross of dirt tracks where people came to buy water from men leading donkeys with barrels on their backs. Shimmering waves of heat rose off the city's few tarmac roads. I saw one or two squalid little shops. Scattered across the endless sand dunes were the houses—invisible behind the tall concrete walls that protected their women from view.

At first I wasn't even aware of what seemed so strange about this country, but then it hit me: Half the population of Saudi Arabia is kept behind walls, all the time. It was hard to fathom a city with almost no women. I felt like a ghost: Women didn't exist, in this world of men. And there were no parks, no flowers, not even any trees. This was a place without color. Apart from the sand, which covered the roads with a soft, dusty carpet, the only colors that stood out were black and white. The men's white thobes, and a very few stark black triangles of cloth: the shrouded women. Geneva was a thousand years away.

A few days later, Yeslam planned an outing for us to the Red Sea, to alleviate our sense of confinement. But the whole experience only emphasized how strange Saudi Arabia really was. My sisters and I had neglected to pack swimsuits. So, in our Western way, we girls debated how and when we should go shopping.

But a Bin Laden woman could not shop—men might see her. So a driver was summoned, and was instructed by the houseboy to get some swimsuits. The driver returned; the houseboy presented us with two suitcases full of various properly modest one-piece suits. This, for many Saudi women at the time, was shopping. Numbed with the strangeness of it all, we selected items we would never ordinarily have dreamt of ever wearing.

We were ready for the beach. I would be meeting some of Yeslam's older brothers for the first time: Omar, a devout, conservative man; Bakr, stern and dour; and Mahrouz, who was becoming increasingly religious, though he had been very Westernized.

The Bin Ladens owned six or seven bungalows by the ocean—rickety little one-room cabins, really, with kitchenettes and a shared generator. The compound was fenced in by cement blocks that stretched right into the sea. The brothers solemnly retired to one cabin; my sisters and I went out to the sea. We lowered ourselves into the water down a rusty ladder off the wooden jetty, and we swam. Om Yeslam watched us, smiling, but ready to warn away any careless man. I'd heard the Red Sea was a scuba diver's paradise; the scenery was beautiful, and it certainly was the bluest blue I'd ever seen a sea. We dressed again, and drank tea, and warm Coke. There were flies everywhere. An effort had been made to amuse us, so we acted amused.

But then Yeslam asked me not to smoke in front of his brothers. It was a trivial request, but after the tension of those first days in Jeddah, I was suddenly overcome with frustration. It seemed that I was to have no say now even in the smallest acts of my daily life. Would I have to deny every detail of my personality in the struggle to fit into this deeply foreign, tightly constraining country? I snapped, "I will not smoke, but I will not marry you either." I meant it—it was the end.

True to his Saudi upbringing, Yeslam avoided an argument. But later, when we were seated together drinking tea, he casually offered me a cigarette in front of his family. That surprising gesture of support gave me hope, and dispelled some of my apprehension about the future. It was a small concession, but I felt it was a symbol. With Yeslam's help and understanding, I would manage to remain myself in this bewildering society.

We made another special excursion, only my third sortie from the house in ten days. Om Yeslam and Yeslam's sister Fawzia took us to the gold souk. It seemed to be one of the only public places a Bin Laden woman ever went to. Walking around in a crowd of faceless, black-shrouded women was an oddly difficult feat. As I looked around me, I realized I couldn't recognize the family—not even my own sisters—amid all the other black triangles walking around. When I dawdled, I had to call out to Fawzia to come and get me.

Gold gleamed everywhere in the souk, bright enough to see even through the dim black face cloth. The shop we went into was tiny, hung from ceiling to floor with gold bracelets and chains and thick rings. These weren't priced by workmanship, but by their weight—they were thrown onto a weighing scale, and then the price was totted up on an abacus. While we were still making our selection, the call rang out for prayer, and the salesmen rushed outside, leaving us there in their shop.

We were not permitted to pray in a public space—we were women. In Saudi Arabia women are forbidden even to step into a mosque, and can only pray in a public space with the ritual prayer that is required in the holy cities of Mecca and Medina. But the male shopkeepers had to pray together when the muezzin called. So they simply left us inside the shop, in a room filled with gold. The door wasn't even locked.

In Saudi Arabia there is hardly any theft. The draconian punishment is a mighty deterrent: Thieves' hands are simply cut off.

The day I got married was the most bizarre moment of those first, strange few weeks. Yeslam and Ibrahim came to take me to the parking lot of an administrative building to register our wedding. I waited, in my abaya, in the car, while they went inside. Yeslam and Ibrahim brought me out a book that I had to sign. It was the marriage register. I was so proud that I had learned to write my name in Arabic letters. Then someone took the book back, and we were married.

I had missed the customary *melka* engagement party, where Regaih had signed her wedding papers amid a ceremonial party of women weeks before. So I got married, in my black abaya, in a sandy parking lot. From the King's permission to a parked car: My wedding had turned out to be so different from what any bride would imagine that it was almost funny. It was as if I was watching someone else get married. I tried to tell myself it didn't really matter.

The double wedding celebration came two days later. We drove to Salem's house, across the road, to get ready. (Many years later I began walking across the road to that house—completely veiled, of course. Such a bold move was the subject of many shocked comments among my female relatives.) There were women everywhere, attended to by armies of hairdressers. I hadn't slept, and I had a crushing headache. One of my sisters told me that the women had handed around my dress in my absence, and had clucked over it before they brought it to me. I suppose it was too simple. I felt scorned, and upset—it seemed so inconsiderate.

I dressed, and my hair was done up in an old-fashioned chignon. I was stiff with nerves. Over my white organza dress went that baleful, stiff black chador. We stepped out to the car in the evening heat; drove to the Candara Hotel. I think it was the only hotel in Jeddah at the time. There, in the garden—strung with naked light bulbs as ersatz fairy-lights—a separate women's area had been prepared, with jute screens to shield us from the gaze of any passing waiters or male guests.

My eyes met a vast crowd of women. Only women; the men's ceremony was taking place elsewhere. Perhaps six hundred guests were massed together, all decked out with jewelry and flounces, as for a grand ceremonial ball. Customarily, a wedding is the only occasion at which women do not veil their faces despite the presence of a strange man—the groom. Still, though their dresses were by Western designers, most of the women not in Yeslam's immediate family covered their hair with a light headscarf. And a few even wore the full abaya. They greeted us with a hullabaloo of ululating calls. Their eyes scrutinized me as Yeslam and I approached the canopy.

We were seated, with Regaih and her groom, on a raised dais. Each female guest approached us, to be greeted. Only women served at the buffet. A women-only orchestra from Kuwait began the monotonous drumming and atonal Arabic music that I learned, over the subsequent years, to appreciate. The women danced the old Bedouin dances in their formal, Western dresses. It is like belly-dancing from Egypt but jerkier, without the lascivious overtones. We sat, under the canopy, on our throne, watching the women. They looked askance at my sisters in their salmon-pink dresses: It was only then that I realized there are no bridesmaids at a Saudi wedding. My headache drummed at me.

Everyone smiled. At no time in my years in Saudi Arabia did I ever feel any direct hostility. A properly brought-up Saudi is never openly rude—except to a servant. Still, I always knew that I was under intense scrutiny. I and my way of life were as strange to them as they were to me. I was a foreigner. I had been brought up in the West, with my face displayed to all. They had been born in the land of Islam's holiest sites—the homeland of the Prophet Mohamed. They believed they were the chosen guardians of the world's most sacred places. They were the chosen people of God.

As I watched them watching me, all the new, and strange, and sometimes unpleasant experiences of those first days in Saudi Arabia struck me with full force. I was married now, to a man from a country that I now realized was very different from my own. Perhaps every bride asks herself if she has made the right decision; I wondered if I should not have asked myself this earlier. Sitting up there, with only women at my feet, I felt overwhelmed by a sense of the enormous gap between two civilizations: the world I came from, and the one that I had just entered. The only thing that eased my restlessness, and my feeling of being confined, was the knowledge that I would soon return to the blessed normality of America. That night, on another planet, President Nixon resigned.

CHAPTER 5

America

THAT FIRST, SURREAL THREE-WEEK VISIT SHOULD have warned me of all the difficulties that would lie ahead. It foreshadowed the coming decades, and would forever change the course of my life. But I was young then, and heedless. When we left Saudi Arabia, a few days after our wedding party, I felt as if I had escaped. The dull haze in my brain was soon dispelled. I scrunched up my abaya and tossed it somewhere, and it was as if nothing had happened: Our new American independence engulfed us again.

We attended classes, shopped for our new home, ate in restaurants, went to movies. We spent time with Mary Martha and her family and socialized with other American friends, which was great for Yeslam's burgeoning business. He had managed to fix his schedule so that he attended classes only two days a week, and spent much of the rest of the week exploring opportunities in the new world of personal computers. I took advantage of everything the American way of life could offer me. I was a married woman now, and in charge of my own life: I could do as I pleased, I thought blithely.

I learned to drive in Yeslam's white sports car, and he bought me a Pontiac Firebird. Like Yeslam, I loved to drive—loved simply driving about when I felt restless. Then Yeslam bought a little Mooney single-engine plane. He persuaded me to take flying lessons. We flew to Santa Barbara together on weekends, and to Las Vegas.

One time Yeslam won big at the casino and he bought me a white mink stole—not that he was really a gambler, but sometimes he enjoyed fooling around. He also bought me jewelry. I loved the attention and the romance of it all as much as the presents themselves.

I think Yeslam was happy then. Happier, certainly, than he'd been in his lonely childhood at boarding schools, far from home, and perhaps happier than he ever was again. We read books together, and stayed up late at night talking about his studies, his first steps in business, listening to the classical music that he loved as loud as we liked. Yeslam had bought one of the first personal computers; he sensed a vast potential for investment and business opportunities in that field. He had been to visit a man called Steve Jobs, who was doing something bold and new with computers in his garage. It was all so exciting to us. We shared everything in this brand-new America that we were free, now, to discover. We were giddy with the open-endedness of it all.

Ibrahim came to live with us, and attended classes at USC, though he was so lackadaisical about studying that I'm not certain he ever graduated. It made Yeslam, so clever and serious, even more attractive to me. Some of Yeslam's other brothers began visiting us, too, on trips abroad, and we would take them to Disneyland, to Las Vegas, to parties. I wore jeans and sneakers; they wore tight trousers and un-buttoned shirts and had Afro hair. They looked just like Americans—on the outside.

Occasionally, Saudi Arabia would come into focus again. Mafouz, Yeslam's milk brother, came to visit us. His mother, Aïsha, was Sheikh Mohamed's oldest child, and she had given birth to Mafouz just as Yeslam's mother was hav-ing her first son. Aïsha and Om Yeslam breast-fed each other's children—it is a custom in Saudi Arabia, though it must never be done if the children are boy and girl, be-cause it would mean they can never marry. To be a milk brother creates a special tie.

Mafouz was deeply devout. In Saudi Arabia he wore his thobe short to display his simplicity—that was the sign of the religious man in those days. This was his first trip abroad. Yeslam took him up in his little airplane for a joy ride, with my sister Salomé. Mafouz spent the whole trip scrunched up in a corner. The seats were close together, and he felt self-conscious and physically repelled, sitting next to a woman who wasn't his relative. His dismay was twofold when Salomé announced that she wasn't feeling well. Poor Mafouz.

In November I realized I was pregnant—the traditional way: I sent Yeslam out again and again for tacos one Sunday morning, and ate myself sick. (I could never bring myself to eat another taco.) I felt surprised that I was really grown-up enough to be expecting a baby, and I was nauseated all the time. Yeslam was glad, of course, and he smiled when I told him, pulling at his little goatee. But he didn't seem as delighted as I'd expected. He was not overwhelmed with joy. He rarely cuddled my tummy or volunteered his amazement when the baby kicked.

We wanted a son—we both knew that. In a household of women, my sisters and I had always been restricted as children. I had often wished I had a brother—I always felt that a brother would have more freedom, and influence my mother to be less strict. And of course Yeslam wanted a boy because he was Saudi: It was as simple as that. Perhaps because of my Iranian background, I understood this without it having to be said.

I had to quit school, on doctor's orders, and rest for much of my pregnancy. An American friend of mine, Billy, came to visit. We'd met in Geneva and had always been close. I looked forward to his visit after days of sitting around the house. My swollen belly was so new: What other topic of conversation could there be? I told Billy we hoped for a boy, but Billy said, "I hope it's a girl. And I hope she'll be just like you. That would be great."

I looked up at Yeslam, smiling. But his face had gone dark. He stared at Billy, not frowning, but he was very still and quiet. Billy left rather quickly. He visited again, but Yeslam managed wordlessly to communicate that Billy was no longer welcome.

In the beginning, you don't see that you're becoming someone else's object. You meet someone and the two of you become one, melding your tastes and personalities until you feel you are invincible. You begin to mute your disagreements, until slowly your own personality becomes submerged in your desire to please. You lose yourself inside the other—the more so if you are from two different cultures, as Yeslam and I were. Pregnancy made me vulnerable, too; and also youth. It happened so gradually that I couldn't even feel it, but my own personality had begun giving way to Yeslam.

Mary Martha was a lifeline in those long months of pregnancy. I felt sick all the time and for months I couldn't even step into a car. Mary Martha helped Yeslam hunt for a new, larger house, in Pacific Palisades. She drove me around to buy baby clothes, and a crib. She took me to my Lamaze preparation classes, and let me prattle on about the little boy I dreamed of.

One time, Mary Martha was organizing a big charity lunch and could find no helpers, so I rounded up the Bin Ladens. Ibrahim, with his huge shaggy Afro, waited tables; Yeslam took the money at the door. I, in my expensive silk pregnancy dress, washed the dishes. As she was leaving, one conservative Californian matron took Mary Martha aside. "Those certainly are some *different* people you have helping you," she said in a loud stage whisper. "Where on earth did you find them?"

"Never mind, you could never afford them," Mary Martha whispered back. In the kitchen, we were weak with laughter.

Mary Martha's family practically adopted us: I had an American family now. When her parents visited from Arizona, we would always go to see them. Her father, Les Barkley, had a big agricultural business cultivating iceberg lettuce—he was a big, strong John Wayne figure. Mary

Martha's mother, Mrs. Barkley, was a gracious, intelligent woman, a firm Republican, with a deep sense of honor. We talked about American politics, and the American Constitution, and about family. We used to do the *Reader's Digest* vocabulary tests together. For her, this was a distraction; for me, essential training.

There was a huge amount of love among the members of Mary Martha's family, and a sense of mutual respect that was new to me. Growing up in my mother's house in Switzerland, I was used to obeying older people unquestioningly—just because they were older. I gave automatic respect and obedience to age and authority. But in Mary Martha's family there was deep acceptance of all the family members. They were well mannered, but they were also free to speak as they wished—free to disagree.

Being with the Barkleys was a warm and welcoming experience. In that family, every individual was respected, regardless of age. Even a child's opinion was listened to, and carefully acknowledged. Their politeness was not mechanical; it was thoughtful. This was the point of view I took with me later, to Saudi Arabia. I strove to bring up my daughters in this spirit. Every day, I grew more strongly anchored to the values of this new, free culture: America.

One March morning in 1975, Yeslam woke me with the news that King Faisal had been assassinated—shot by one of his own nephews. I could feel his sense of panic and urgency. Saudi Arabia was in an uproar, Yeslam told me. It was claimed that the assassin was deranged, but most likely it was a revenge killing, Yeslam said: The murderer's brother had been executed ten years previously for participating in an Islamic fundamentalist revolt against the King's decision to authorize television in the Kingdom.

Increasingly, Yeslam felt he needed to return to his country and help with the family business. He began rushing through his studies so he could graduate early.

I, meanwhile, gave birth—the most momentous event in my life, and one that would change me forever. Mary Martha was with me. (I felt Yeslam would not be able to handle the gory details.) The baby was a girl.

Much later, I learned that Yeslam simply walked out when he learned that—turned on his heel and walked out of the hospital. But at the time, I was exhausted. When they installed me in my room, and brought me my new baby, all I knew was that Yeslam was there. I thought that perhaps he was a little disappointed, but I was sure we would adjust.

Now we would have to pick out a name. We'd chosen a boy's name—Faisal—but we had never gotten around to choosing one for a girl. Yeslam settled on Wafah, the faithful one.

Having a girl came as such a surprise to me; and what a nice surprise she would turn out to be. Wafah was beautiful—really unusually good-looking for a newborn—and when I looked at her I couldn't possibly be disappointed. I was overwhelmed with fascination and love. But Yeslam was petulant at times. It was almost as if he was jealous of the hold that little Wafah had on me. Although he came from a large family he was much less attentive to Wafah than I was. He acted happy when I pointed out the new things she was doing—sucking her toes or reaching out for toys—but I did always have to point them out.

Soon after Wafah was born, Mary Martha took me out to go shopping. I thought it would be good for Yeslam to bond with the baby alone. Wafah still needed to be fed every two hours, so we raced around buying baby clothes. When we came back, Yeslam held her out to me, like a package. "She's wet," he said. "You should change her."

Yeslam was so silly, I mused. Hadn't it occurred to him to change her himself? I felt so tender toward him. His haplessness made me feel even more confident and capable in my new role as a mother.

For me, Wafah was like a miracle. For the first time in my life I was completely responsible for another human being. Like all new mothers, I promised myself I wouldn't make the same mistakes my own mother had. I would respect my baby's character and let her grow, free to become whatever person already lay, furled up, inside her perfect little body.

I didn't want to hire a nanny (though we did, at that point, have a maid to cook and clean). It was I who woke up to feed Wafah at night, though Yeslam grumbled. I propped Wafah up beside me and talked to her all day long. She'd look back at me, clear-eyed, as if she'd understood every word.

I truly enjoyed walking my baby through the park in her new American buggy, playing with her in the sunlight, smelling the wonderful babyness in the folds of her neck. She was a stubborn little thing, with a fiercely strong character. For months after she was weaned she refused to eat anything except ready-made Gerber Turkey and Rice dinners, and even Mary Martha's good home cooking couldn't tempt her.

I flooded our house with music—Cat Stevens, Shirley Bassey, Charles Aznavour, Jacques Brel—twirling my lovely little girl around the living room. She went to sleep accompanied by Tchaikovsky on her own hi-fi system, surrounded by a department store's worth of toys. Nothing was too good for my Wafah.

I didn't return to college, though I lived through every term paper and exam at Yeslam's side as he raced through the syllabus. His mind was quick and incisive. I adored his intelligence, his discipline, his rapid grasp of complex facts. As his graduation came closer, his plans to take us back to Saudi Arabia became more urgent. After the oil embargo of 1973, when the price of crude oil rose from about $3 to $12 in the space of a few months, money had begun pouring into Saudi Arabia. Yeslam realized that new opportunities for business were opening up, and he wanted to be a part of it. He told me it would be great for our new family. I knew it meant renouncing my hopes to return to college—that it meant renouncing many things—but, lulled in my cozy joy at life with my beloved little Wafah and my clever, handsome husband, I agreed.

Carmen, age six, on
holiday in Persia, now Iran

*I was brought up in
Switzerland but spent my
holidays in Persia, visiting
my mother's family.*

Carmen, age fourteen

*My mother was a stickler for
appearances and until I
rebelled she used to dress all
four of us girls exactly alike.*

1973, in my mother's garden in Geneva

The summer I met Yeslam, young people ruled the world. I was excited about my future and very much in love.

In Geneva, my sisters Magnolia, Salomé, and Béatrice with our maternal aunt and her two children

Yeslam's brother Ibrahim and their father Sheikh Mohamed, in Jeddah in the 1950s

Sheikh Mohamed had fifty-four children in all. He was a formidable man and I still keep a photo of him in my living room in Geneva.

Some of Yeslam's family, on a trip to the Pacific Palisades. Ahmad, Shafik, Ragaih, Yahla, Yeslam, and Ahmad

With their jeans and their Afro hair, they looked just like any American— on the outside.

1973, Interlaken, Switzerland. At tea with Yeslam, his mother Om Yeslam, and his sister Fawzia

More and more often Yeslam included me in his family outings.

Saudi women did not have photos in their passports, but as a foreigner I needed one for my visa. My face had to be visible but, naturally, I wore the headscarf.

1974, Jeddah

Since cameras were very unusual in Saudi Arabia at the time, I have only a few amateurish snapshots of my actual wedding. So, the following day, we took some shots. Whereas the day before Yeslam had been in full traditional costume, here he is wearing a Western suit.

Yeslam and his brother Ibrahim, the day after the wedding celebration

It was rare to have so many flowers in Jeddah at the time.

1974, Yeslam and me in California

It was our first trip to the States. America was like a dream come true for me, incredibly open, truly a land of opportunity.

1976, in Santa Monica, with Yeslam, Fawzia, Om Yeslam, Mary Martha, and Wafah

Yeslam bought a little Mooney single-engine plane. I took flying lessons.

With Wafah at three
months old

*The birth of my first
little girl was the most
momentous event of my
life. It changed me
completely as a person.*

Mary Martha
with Wafah on
her first birthday

*Mary Martha has been
my dearest friend, my
mentor, and a constant
source of inspiration
and comfort. I called her
my American Mom.*

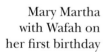

1976, in Santa Monica
with Wafah and Yeslam

*I was so happy with my
beautiful baby and my
clever, handsome husband.
Life seemed full of possibility.*

1976, USC on Yeslam's
graduation day

*I had encouraged Yeslam
to study, and even though
I had had to give up school
myself I was thrilled when
he graduated.*

CHAPTER 6

Life with the Bin Ladens

WE MOVED TO JEDDAH IN THE FALL OF 1976. THIS time, as we circled the airport, I had a proper, thin silk Saudi abaya to put over my head, my eyes, my hands, every inch of my body. But the heavy feeling that I had forgotten, returned as I cloaked myself in the impenetrable gauze, and this time it felt stronger. I would not be leaving after two weeks. This was not a veil that I could one day scrunch up in a ball and forget at the back of a closet. This abaya would now accompany me everywhere. In this new, strange country, the abaya would symbolize my life.

For years, the first thing people asked me when I traveled abroad was "Do you wear the veil?" And when I said yes, I always used to get a kick out of how astonished and appalled they were. Of course, in practical terms, the veil was an inconvenience. It was an insult to my intelligence and to my freedom. But I didn't make a big drama out of it. To cover my unease, in those early days, I accepted the Saudi explanation that the abaya symbolized respect for women. More fundamentally, I was convinced that it would be temporary.

I am an optimist by nature. Jeddah was booming, and foreigners had begun flocking to the country. The menacing emptiness of the desert all around would soon give way to vast new roads and shiny skyscrapers. I assumed that Saudi society would move into the modern world, just as other cultures had.

Soon, I thought—as in Iran—the veil would be something that women could choose to wear—or not. We would soon, as a matter of course, be able to walk around the streets. Or drive where we wanted. We would shop on our own: There would soon be stores. We would work, if we wished to.

Meanwhile, I had to adjust to my new life, and try to become a good Saudi wife and mother. We moved in with Om Yeslam and Yeslam's younger sister Fawzia. I shared Om Yeslam's Sudanese driver, Abdou; we hired another Ethiopian maid.

I tried to adjust. I gradually picked up basic Arabic, and as Wafah cut her teeth and toddled about I found motherhood absorbing. Other than that, nothing about my new life came naturally.

Strangest of all was becoming enfolded into Om Yeslam's quiet, unhurried life, into her woman's world. It was like going under an anesthetic. Om Yeslam was a good woman, but her only interests were cooking and the Koran. She prayed five times a day, and she lived in a world that was strictly bound by an invisible cage of tradition.

The Arabic word for woman, *hormah*, derives from the word *haram*: sin; and every moment of Om Yeslam's life was intertwined with her observation of the rituals and rules of

Islamic custom. Everything seemed to be *haram*, or sinful; and if it wasn't sinful it was *abe*, shameful. It was *haram* to play music, *abe* to walk around in the street; *abe* to talk to a male servant, *haram* to be seen by a man outside the family. Om Yeslam was a tolerant woman, and her still, calm face rarely frowned, but I could infer her disapproval of my behavior from her always politely voiced surprise.

It was, of course, almost always *haram* and *abe* for a Bin Laden woman to leave the house. Our faces could never be seen by a man outside the family. If we left the house, it was to be driven somewhere specific, by a man. It was months before I even understood the layout of the neighborhood.

Shopping was for servants. If we needed something, Abdou or another driver would have to be instructed by the houseboy to search for the required item. It wasn't just swimsuits. It was tea, or sanitary napkins—anything at all. If we didn't like them, he would return with another suitcaseful. We would select something, he would go back to the shop with the suitcase, ascertain the price, and return again for the payment.

These rigmaroles drove me insane.

The system that constricted all women in a mesh of restraints made every basic gesture of my life unbelievably complex. Wafah was accustomed to drinking Similac baby milk. Though I'd brought a large stock, it was running out. I was concerned that she might be allergic to other brands—I felt she lacked energy, though perhaps it was the heat. I was determined to find Similac for her. I sent Abdou out for some, but he returned time and again with a barrel of basic baby milk—not the right kind.

Finding Similac became obsessively important to me. I couldn't imagine that there were only two kinds of baby milk available in the entire country. One night, I told Yeslam he absolutely had to let me go to the grocery store so that I could check myself. He acquiesced.

I would go to the grocery store! What a step forward! I was jubilant. Abdou and Yeslam drove me there, abaya-ed from head to toe. Yeslam asked me to wait in the car, and disappeared for a while. Finally, after ten minutes he guided me to the entrance.

I walked past a line of about a dozen men standing outside the door, all stiffly facing away from me. Once I stepped inside, my hopes crumbled. The store was a shabby, windowless prefab, dusty and crowded with cardboard boxes filled with cans. It smelled like a warehouse. Even finding the milk was difficult—everything was in unlabeled boxes. There was hardly any choice, and certainly no Similac. And in order that one completely black-shrouded woman could walk inside with her husband, the store had been emptied—completely emptied—of all its clients and staff.

What on earth did they fear—contamination? From one woman, whose face and body could not even be seen? Could it really be a sign of politeness and respect for these men to turn their backs on me because I was a woman? I was overcome with rage. Just a few weeks before, I had raced through a brightly lit California supermarket grabbing fresh fruit and cereal for my family. I returned home, a bitter knot of hopeless homesickness in the pit of my stomach. I felt I'd entered an alien, parallel universe.

I needed activity. I needed to read. I longed for some

stimulation of my mind, and my body. The two TV channels broadcast an imam chanting the Koran all day; for lighter fare, little boys as young as six or seven, who had won prizes for their Koranic knowledge, recited the holy texts from memory. Foreign newspapers were Magic Markered into fragments: Any comment on Saudi Arabia or Israel, any photo or advertisement showing even one inch of a woman's limbs or neck was blacked out by the censors. I held them up to the light, to divine the forbidden words veiled by the censor's pen.

There were no books. There were no theaters, no concerts, no cinemas. There was no reason to go out, and in any case we could not go out: I was not allowed to go for a walk, and legally could not drive. Much as I loved my role as a mother, taking care of Wafah was not enough to fill my mind and my days.

I had to get out. I told Yeslam I was desperate. He understood—he proposed we make a three-day trip to Geneva to buy books, and some baby milk, and to assuage my homesickness. As often happened during those first few years in Saudi Arabia, when I forced myself to complain, Yeslam found a way to reassure me. I revived: My husband was on my side.

In Geneva, my familiar world looked startlingly different. I gazed at it all with new eyes. Suddenly everything I had taken for granted all my life seemed marvelous. Just five hours away from the brown, dry, vacant land around the Jeddah airport, here was a complex landscape filled with life. There were so many houses and people, such richly colored fields and gardens. I found myself staring at the sharp blue-gray mountains, trying to memorize each jagged edge. Even the trees in my mother's garden seemed powerfully significant. I stared at the shapes and colors of the red autumn leaves, soaking them into my brain. It was as though I was seeing them for the first time.

I bought piles of books and basic supplies. Then I steeled myself for our return.

During our first year in Saudi Arabia, Yeslam traveled often for his first job in his family's corporation. He went mostly to Dammam, a rapidly developing port on the eastern coast that had been built to serve the oil industry. Staying alone in Jeddah for two or three days at a time, with Om Yeslam and Fawzia my only adult companions, drove me half-mad with boredom—with or without my stash of books.

I spent most of my days alone with Om Yeslam. Fawzia attended classes at the university—she was studying business—but it was not like any university I had ever imagined. Her "classes" were in reality video presentations by male professors who could not be permitted to teach directly in a strictly segregated, women-only classroom. There was a library, but women students had to apply for books in writing, and received them from a office reserved for that purpose a week later. I never saw Fawzia read a book, or heard her talk about her studies.

I could feel myself sinking into lassitude. I felt bored and aimless as a goldfish, swimming slower and slower inside an absolutely smooth glass bowl, with nothing to do, gulping for air.

The heat crushed us all into submission. During the day we never left the air-conditioned house. Stepping out into the garden at dusk was like walking into a furnace. The first time I saw Om Yeslam animated was when it rained. We woke up one morning to a gray sky, and everyone talked excitedly about the coming rain. As the first droplets fell, Om Yeslam and Fawzia rushed out into the garden. "It's raining, it's raining," they cried. "Come out and see." I knew what rain was—this at last was something I knew very well—but to please them I emerged. The wet sand smelled unpleasant, but it didn't matter: It was raining and that made them happy. The garden flooded, with a foot or so of water washing around the concrete walls. For a couple of days the sand grew green, as if even the desert was grateful.

Later, I, too, would dash out into the rain, for joy at some slight change in the routine of my life.

The sandstorms were less pleasant. Sharp shards of sand would be whipped up by a wheeling, cutting wind. The sky would darken, sometimes for days. Clouds of dust entered everywhere, through closed doors and windows, creeping into your clothes, your shoes, your food. It was uncomfortable and frightening; the noise was sinister. I never grew accustomed to it.

Afterward the gardener would sweep the sand back into the desert, a futile gesture that always gave me pause. We were living in a place that was never meant for human habitation. Though Jeddah is on the sea—it is a major port—the desert is ever-present, stony and wild, constantly encroaching on life. It has not even one river, no gentle natural greens, no mellow colors.

The desert of Saudi Arabia is beautiful, in a way: The wavy sand dunes, the striking light, and the wide, vast horizon made me think of the ocean. But it is immense and monotonous—utterly empty. A kingdom carved from the desert is a forbidding place. Until the nineteenth century no European had ever even entered the vast, isolated desert that is Saudi Arabia. Physically, it is perhaps the most unwelcoming country on the planet.

CHAPTER 7

The Patriarch

SOCIALLY, SAUDI ARABIA IS MEDIEVAL, DARK WITH sin and interdiction. The Saudi version of Islam—Wahabism—is ferocious in its enforcement of a stark and ancient social code. This is not a complex, intellectual culture like that of Iran, or Egypt. The Kingdom was not even fifty years old when I arrived there, and it was—is—very close to its early tribal traditions.

Saudi Arabia may be wealthy, but it is probably the least cultivated country in the rich and multifaceted Arab world, with the most simplistic and brutal conception of social relationships. Families are headed by patriarchs, and obedience to the patriarch is absolute. The only values that count in Saudi Arabia are loyalty and submission—first to Islam, then to the clan.

Yeslam's father, Sheikh Mohamed, was in many ways the archetype of the Saudi patriarch, though he was in fact born in neighboring Yemen. His personality was larger than life; his will was law. Mohamed was a poor worker who had come to Saudi Arabia in the 1930s. The Sheikh had a mind like fire for figures, though he couldn't read or write. Pious, honorable, and scrupulous, and respected by his workforce, Mohamed built a company that grew into one of the largest construction groups in the Middle East, before he died in a plane crash, in 1967, at the age of fifty-nine.

Sheikh Mohamed's relationship with the Saudi royal family dated from the years when King Abdel Aziz, the founder of the Kingdom, was still on the throne. According to a Bin Laden family legend, the ailing King was unable to climb the stairs in one of his palaces. Sheikh Mohamed's crew managed to design and install a special ramp so that the King could be driven by automobile directly up to the second floor.

In another family story, my father-in-law drastically underbid an Italian company that was scheduled to construct the road from Jeddah to hilly Taef, where King Abdel Aziz often spent the summer months. Mohamed followed a mule making the journey, mapped out the animal's trail, and used that path to build the road.

Yeslam's father was a generous man, given to great gestures of abundance. Once, I was told, when spendthrift King Saud was on the throne, Sheikh Mohamed had reached into his own deep pockets and paid the salaries of the government's civil servants to save the Kingdom from financial embarrassment. Another time, a group of poor Indonesians making a pilgrimage to Mecca were left stranded by their guide, without their return tickets or cash. They went to Sheikh Mohamed—the biggest employer in the region—to beg for work, so they could make enough to pay for the airfare home. He simply gave them the money.

Sheikh Mohamed was wily, and brave. He often worked alongside his labor crew: Unlike most wealthy Saudis, he was not averse to manual labor. He willingly endured great hardship. Although I've no idea if the story is true, Yeslam told me that once during the war between Egypt and Yemen, in the 1950s, Sheikh Mohamed and his men worked under fire from the Egyptian air force to complete construction of an airbase in a neighboring region of Saudi Arabia.

This was life on a spectacularly grand scale. And Sheikh Mohamed carried that sense of the spectacular into his home life, too. Islam permits a man to marry four wives, and most Saudis are content to marry one or two—four at most. But, like a few of the royal princes, Sheikh Mohamed swelled the ranks of his wives by divorcing older women and marrying new ones as the whim took him. (Divorce is a simple procedure in Islam—for a man.) When he died, he had amassed twenty-two wives—twenty-one of them still living.

After years of living in Saudi Arabia, I learned from one of his most trusted employees that the night he died, Sheikh Mohamed had been planning to marry a twenty-third wife. He was headed there when his private plane crashed in the desert.

Sheikh Mohamed never actually lived at Kilometer Seven. He lived with most of his wives and children in a huge compound in Jeddah, and maintained smaller establishments in the Saudi capital of Riyadh, and elsewhere. Mohamed's favorite wife, Om Haidar, lived with him in the big house in Jeddah, Yeslam told me, and he rotated nights as he pleased with other wives in smaller houses scattered around inside the high walls of his compound. Cooking and child care were more or less collective, by affinity among the wives, and the current wives had a higher status than the divorced.

Sheikh Mohamed had had fifty-four children. I used to tease Yeslam, saying that his father had been competing with King Saud, who had over one hundred offspring.

All Sheikh Mohamed's children would forever live their lives in the gigantic shadow of their father. To them, he was a hero—a distant, fabled figure, stern and deeply devout. The younger children rarely saw him. From time to time, Yeslam told me, he and his brothers would go to the big house for inspection. Their fearsome father would ask them if they had prayed, or ask them to recite the Koran, and reward them with a coin or a pat.

Sheikh Mohamed fascinated me. A poor, illiterate man from one of the most deprived regions on earth—the Hadramat, in Yemen—he had emigrated to Saudi Arabia, a country bare of any elements of modern civilization. And he had become one of the most powerful men in the Kingdom's fledgling economy. Sheikh Mohamed became a kind of baron in that medieval regime. He was the largest employer in the country. He was befriended and trusted by kings. By any standard, in any culture, Sheikh Mohamed would have been counted a genius.

Sadly, none of his children has ever measured up to Sheikh Mohamed. Yeslam came closest, for his sharp intelligence, but he was panicky and fearful—he didn't have the stature or the strategic vision of his father. Salem let the organization stagnate; Bakr had no drive—he was pedestrian. And Osama? Though he has certainly made the Bin Laden name famous across the world, I would like to believe that his father would not have approved of the way he did it.

Once, Yeslam told me, Tabet was caught out in a lie, and Sheikh Mohamed hit him. Another time, Sheikh Mohamed took one of his older sons to see King Faisal. The King invited the child to come and sit at the King's side in his reception room—he insisted that the boy join him, and designated a place where he should sit—but Mohamed said no. He said no to the King.

While he lived, his sons never disobeyed him, or became involved in disputes with each other. The line of authority was clear: Sheikh Mohamed's word was law.

Sheikh Mohamed was a handsome, energetic man. I still have an imposing portrait of him in my living room today. In his Saudi robes and dark glasses, he gives off an air of panache, strength, and intelligence. His children lived in awe of him. The wives did, too: I rarely met a Saudi woman who was not afraid of her husband. Sheikh Mohamed was not violent, but he had total power over his wives. He could neglect them, or, worse, divorce them. They lived in confinement, utterly dependent on him.

A wife in Saudi Arabia cannot do anything without her husband's permission. She cannot go out, cannot study, often cannot even eat at his table. Women in Saudi Arabia must live in obedience, in isolation, and in the fear that they may be cast out and summarily divorced.

When I arrived in Saudi Arabia, Haidar's mother, the favorite wife, was still living near Kilometer Seven. She was a pretty woman, and a very efficient organizer—with her, Yeslam told me, the house was assured smooth functioning, and his father could relax. Om Haidar was more sophisticated than some of Mohamed's other wives. She was Syrian, and she had great poise. She smiled gently, her voice was melodious, and I believe that Om Yeslam consciously modeled herself on her.

But Om Haidar was not the ruler of the clan. All my mothers-in-law seemed to maintain relationships of perfect harmony with each other, although a few lived in Riyadh and Mecca, and several of the foreign-born wives—those who came from Lebanon, or Egypt, or Ethiopia—moved back and forth between their homelands and Jeddah, where their children lived. Even Salem, the oldest brother, did not seem to issue edicts or rulings, although he was acknowledged as the clan leader, and many of my sisters-in-law—particularly those who had no brothers—depended on him for every major decision about their lives. There was a kind of common, unspoken understanding that ran the family machine without any one driver taking control.

By the time I arrived, seven years after Sheikh Mohamed's death, there were no apparent distinctions between current wives and those who had been divorced. Sheikh Mohamed had, of course, divorced many of them; and one, Om Ali, he remarried after divorcing. His custom was to maintain his divorced wives and their children at his compound so long as the women did not marry another man, as the law permitted them to. If they did—like Om Tareg—he kept the children with him, distributing them to his other wives.

After many years of living in Saudi Arabia I learned that, in addition to maintaining wives and divorced wives, Sheikh Mohamed sometimes chose to establish contracts with semi-wives. The practice of *serah*—what we would call concubines, though the word is not a perfect one—is not well regarded in Saudi Arabia, and it is something you encounter rather rarely, but it has always been legal. Probably because in Islam no child may be illegitimate, it was long ago established that a man could set up a contract with a girl, or her father, for a kind of limited marital arrangement.

The marriage lasts an hour or a lifetime, according to the contract. Whatever the relationship, the semi-wife does not inherit wealth on the man's death. If a child is born he or she is legitimate. Sheikh Mohamed installed these mothers also on his compound, and treated their children exactly as he did the others.

If Sheikh Mohamed cast one of these women out, for whatever reason, he always kept the child. In Saudi Arabia, the head of the family—be that the father or the eldest son—can demand the strictest application of the Sharia Islamic law against a member of the clan. It chilled me whenever I was faced with this. Over the years to come, I met many women who had been completely banished from any contact with their children, even by phone.

As I would learn, if a child flouts the harsh customs and conventions, the patriarch may even put that child to death.

CHAPTER 8

Life as an Alien

I NEVITABLY, AS THE MONTHS WENT BY I BEGAN TO settle into my new life. I started to think about the future. Musing about redecorating the house was a recurrent fantasy: I was enclosed there night and day—often for weeks at a time—and the decor was truly hideous.

I tried to keep myself busy, reading, playing with Wafah. One day, Yeslam's younger brother Osama came to visit. Today, of course, he is by far the most notorious of Yeslam's brothers. Back then, however, he was a minor figure: a young student attending King Abdel Aziz University in Jeddah, respected in the family for his stern religious beliefs, and recently married to a Syrian niece of his mother's.

Osama was perfectly integrated into the family, although he didn't live at Kilometer Seven. He was a tall man, despite the slightness of his build, and he had a commanding presence—when Osama stepped into the room, you felt it. But he was not strikingly different from the other brothers—just younger, and more reserved. That afternoon I was playing with Wafah, in the hallway, and when the doorbell rang, I stupidly, automatically, answered it myself, instead of calling for the houseboy.

Catching sight of Osama and Aïsha's son Mafouz, I smiled and asked them in. "Yeslam is here," I assured them. But Osama snapped his head away when he saw me, and glared back toward the gate. "No, really," I insisted. "Come in." Osama was making rapid back-off gestures with his hand, waving me aside, muttering something in Arabic, but I truly didn't understand what he meant. Mafouz could see that I was seemingly lacking in the basics of social etiquette, and he finally explained that Osama could not see my naked face.

In Saudi culture, any man who might one day become your husband is not supposed to see you unveiled. The only men who may look at a woman's face are her father, her brothers, her husband, her stepfather. Osama was among those men who followed the rule strictly. So I retreated into a back room while my admirably devout brother-in-law visited my husband. I felt stupid and awkward.

Years later, I was amazed to read in the Western press that Osama had been a playboy as a teenager in Beirut. I think if it were true, I would have heard about it. Another brother-in-law, Mahrouz, did have that reputation: He had chased many a skirt while studying in Lebanon, but later he changed, and he was now a strictly religious man. I never heard such tales about Osama, however. The now famous photographs that were taken of a crowd of teenaged Bin Laden brothers in Sweden—they don't show Osama either. At the time, I think, Osama was in Syria. The boy identified in the media as Osama is in fact another brother.

As far as I know, Osama was always devout. His family revered him for his piety. Never once did I hear anyone murmur that his fervor might be a little excessive, or perhaps a passing phase.

The Bin Ladens were all religious, though their piety varied in degree. Men like Osama and Mahrouz were the most extreme. Bakr was devout, but not repressive. Like many young Saudi men, Yeslam, Salem, and another brother, Hassan, were more casual about their practice of Islam, although as they aged, religion seemed to catch up with them.

The Bin Laden men could choose to be a little more flexible about their religious observance: That was their right. But it did not extend to the women. All the women in the Bin Laden family were very proper, and in Saudi Arabia that meant they were devout. When Yeslam's brother Hassan married a Lebanese girl, there was widespread gossip about her former job as an airline hostess. Leila confided in me that she felt her mother-in-law would never approve of her. She suffered from the disapproval of the family.

I sought to please. I couldn't rid myself of the awareness of how disappointed Om Yeslam must have been that her son had married a foreigner. I tried to control my impetuous nature. I tried to learn to pray: the ritual washing; wrapping every inch of myself in a light sheet; performing the ballet of kneeling, bowing, and standing while facing Mecca, Islam's holiest place. But I never could seem to manage to pray five times a day, as most of the other Bin Laden women did.

The Bin Ladens were deeply proud of the Mecca shrine, like all Saudis. They are steeped from childhood in the honor and responsibility of caring for Mecca, where the Prophet

Mohamed was inspired by Allah. And the Saudi form of Islam is the strictest—they would say purest—form that religion can take. In the 1700s an itinerant preacher called Sheikh Mohamed bin Abdul Wahab—a kind of Muslim puritan revivalist—became inspired by his revulsion at the people's mixture of Islam with old prayers to sacred stones and trees, and their shrines to holy men. Abdel Aziz ibn Saud, then a desert warlord, was inspired by the teachings of Sheikh Wahab to conquer and unify the whole of Saudi Arabia, in 1932.

This is how Saudi Arabia became the only country in the world to take the name of its ruling kings, the al-Sauds. They established Saudi Arabia—with some help from the British—wielding the sword and the Word. Their control of a vast country of separate Bedouin tribes was cemented by imposing absolute obedience to Sheikh Wahab's strict Koranic rules, in order to preserve the holiness of Mecca.

Mohamed Bin Laden was so pious, and so beloved by the King, that his company, the Bin Laden Organization, was given the exclusive right to renovate Mecca and Medina, Islam's second holiest city. It is hard to convey the honor that this reflected on his family. It was no wonder that his wives were so religious—though sometimes it was hard for me to bear.

I went to Mecca for the first time with a female acquaintance of Kuwaiti origin. On the road, we passed huge billboards warning non-Muslims to turn back. We came to an inspection post: Saudi officials are obsessive about forbidding non-Muslims to soil the Mecca holy sites. It made me nervous. My mother was born a Muslim, but her practice of

Islam was certainly questionable in the light of the Bin Ladens' piety. And my father had been a Christian—something I never hid, but always felt I should. I had learned how to pray, certainly, but I didn't really feel I was a proper Muslim. Still, Abdou drove us through, cheerfully—"Bin Laden" was all he said to the inspection official, and of course that was enough. We arrived just as the cry to prayer rang out, and I started nervously performing the prayer ritual.

An official from the terrifying religious police, the mutawa, immediately began yelling at me, and I panicked. Had I made some crucial error in the ritual—something that betrayed my inexperience? Would I be disowned as an impostor? But Abdou told me I was praying in the men's area. It hadn't even occurred to me that we would be kept separate, even here. Nothing comes easily, I thought, trying to breathe through my sudden fear.

We went a little further along, to the section of the huge courtyard that is reserved for women. We prayed. We walked the seven turns, and drank the waters of the Zamzam, where three millennia ago Abraham's second wife, Hagar, was directed by God to find water for her young son Ishmael, father of the Arabs. We touched the Ka'aba, the black stone that God gave Abraham, which so many millions of hands had touched before us. We saw the locked door that led to the closed room which is the holy place inside the holy place—a room where Yeslam and other Bin Laden men had been permitted to pray.

Philosophically I have always felt that it doesn't matter how you pray to God or what texts you read—the Bible, the Koran, the Torah. But in that colossal, holy place of tradition, toward which one billion Muslims turn in prayer every day, even I felt a spiritual charge.

I went home thoughtful. I was greeted by Yeslam's unbounded delight. It was not the sacred hajj period, but I had accomplished the umra, the lesser pilgrimage to Mecca, without the millions of pilgrims who converge on the city during hajj time. "I've told everyone that you have done the umra!" he crowed. He seemed so proud of me. When I told him about the mutawa, he started laughing.

We started going out occasionally, seeing other couples. Some of them were among the expatriate bankers and industrialists who had begun arriving en masse to Saudi Arabia to take part in the great boom. One or two were modern-thinking Saudis, who could bear to see an unveiled woman's face—and, more shocking still, dine with her at table. I felt inspired by these moments of normality—though I would almost always discover that these were not truly Saudi households: The wives were invariably from elsewhere, Syria or Egypt or Lebanon.

After one such dinner, on our late drive home, Yeslam gestured me to sit with him in the front of the car. And then he said I could take off the veil and bare my face, if I wished. Of course I wished! I sat there watching the streetlights clearly, unveiled outside for the first time.

It felt like another milestone. Months ago I had moved around with two folds of veil over my eyes and my whole face; I had to sit in the back of the car, and nobody spoke to me in public. Now I was permitted to eat at the table of a man outside the Bin Laden family. I sat beside my husband in the car, and I could see the streetlights undimmed by the veil. I needed to count these little victories. I clutched at these small signals of change. I felt they were carrying me forward.

I realize now that the bars of my cage were only moving a little wider. But at the time it seemed as if the door to freedom and choice was starting to creak open.

Sometimes it all seemed to be moving so slowly, and I would be overcome with despair. And yet I stayed, always. I realized that in some sense I was privileged. I was living a unique moment in the evolution of the country. Saudi Arabia was speeding away from the Middle Ages and making huge leaps ahead in material progress. Naively, I believed that economic change would be followed by social shifts, too, which would alter beyond recognition the lot of Saudi women. I thought I could participate in that essential moment in history. I was at the crucial place, at the crucial time. The prospect of being part of the tremendous social changes that I believed were on the way—that was thrilling.

And yet nothing seemed to change for the women in the Bin Laden family. Their lives were so constrained—so small, and faded—that it frightened me. They never left their houses alone. They never did anything. Their only goal in life seemed to be to adhere more perfectly to the most restrictive rules of Islam. Even if I'd tried, I could not have lived like that, and I certainly did not aspire to.

The Bin Laden women were like pets kept by their husbands. They were kept shut in their homes, or occasionally accompanied out on special outings. All day long they waited for their husbands to come back—all night long, too, sometimes—and when they did, the wives would perform their role as joyful, welcoming companions. Occasionally they were patted on the head and given presents; sometimes they were taken out, mostly to each other's houses.

Preparing these little parties was the women's only occupation; that, and the elaborate preening and fussing with their formal, frilly clothes that happened beforehand. Every tea party was the same. We seated ourselves stiffly on uncomfortable chairs. There was no small talk or deeper discussion, a lot of silence, and little cups of tea and coffee with different kinds of cakes. Talk centered on their children—who meanwhile spent most of their time with foreign maids—and on the Koran. Sometimes we talked about clothes.

I had the impression that none of the women ever read, except perhaps the Koran and other works of Koranic interpretation. I never once saw one of my sisters-in-law pick up a book. These women never met with men other than their husbands, and never talked about larger issues even with the men they had married. They had nothing to say. We talked about the health of our husbands and children, and they made constant, quite kindly efforts to make a good Muslim out of me. As time went on, I did come to see the presence of some of them as a welcome distraction. Mostly, though, they bored me to tears.

Yeslam did not treat me as his brothers did their wives. If he had, I could not have borne living in Saudi Arabia. But in those days my husband was very different from other Saudi men. He treated me like a Western man would—more or less as his equal. Yeslam involved me in his life and thoughts. He enjoyed my mind, and he sought my advice. We talked about everything, all the time. He wanted me to be his partner, a full member of a two-person team.

It became a kind of ritual—we would talk together while Yeslam showered, after he came home from work, around two or three. We talked about his day, what I'd been reading, things in the news—it seemed we never stopped talking. We spent afternoons and evenings plunged in discussion. Often the subject was politics. On a daily basis, Yeslam confided in me his troubles at the Bin Laden Organization—changes that he planned, or his worries for the company's future, the intrigues and the often nasty bickering and infighting of his apparently calm brothers.

Yeslam had a strange relationship with his brothers. On the one hand, they were his only companions—he had no male friends to speak of. His family members were the only people who counted in Yeslam's life. There is a Saudi saying, "Me and my cousin against the stranger; me and my brother against my cousin." Among nomads—and Saudi culture was formed by desert nomads—the clan is the only unit that makes sense. So Yeslam did trust his brothers more than most people in the West trust their family. He knew he could count on them to some extent. But with me, he could confide his frustrations with his clan—his brothers' petty squabbles, and their many hidden power struggles.

Sometimes I would look over at Yeslam, as we were playing cards or backgammon in the evening, or listening to music together, and I would catch my breath. He was so beautiful, with his fine features and gentle eyes. And he needed me. I knew he loved me. To him I was his strength—

his equal—a completely loyal partner who put herself aside so that he could go forward.

In that, I think, Yeslam was unique in Saudi Arabia. The lowliness and subservience of Saudi women is deeply inscribed in that culture. Pleasure, comfort, equality—so many things I had taken for granted were completely foreign here. This was not like the way of life in Persia, or in other Arab countries. Saudi society is very close to its roots in the ancient codes of the Bedouin, who have always lived as nomads in a vast desert that has kept them isolated from the rich cultures around them. Saudi Arabia is a stern, implacable country. For many Saudis, it seems sometimes, almost every kind of pleasure is a sin.

I was very young then, and I believed things would change. I lived for Yeslam and Wafah, and I lived for the future. I thought that with Yeslam's intelligence and his family's power, we could help change things. I clutched at every sign that Saudi Arabia was entering the modern world: a lifted veil seen on the street; a new, women-only bank that meant women could have their own bank accounts; an English-language TV channel; a new bookstore.

I was almost always disappointed. The English-language TV channel was censored to shreds. Apart from news of the King's latest foreign visit, it mostly showed cartoons and the cop show *Columbo*—shows with no kissing or politics. The bookstore sold almost no books: Saudi Arabian customs officials would not permit entry to any love stories, or books by Jews, or to most books on religion, Middle Eastern politics, or Israel. It was dispiriting, but again, I assumed it was just a matter of time before things would change.

Nobody at that time could have even imagined that Saudi Arabia would in fact become more fanatically religious, more oppressively conservative, as the years went by. But countries go through phases, like people. So many Saudi men perform this cycle. When they are young they are thoughtless—they take what is comfortable and amusing in Western culture—but then they marry. Underneath they have always maintained their self-assured and inflexible value system, and it rises to the surface as they age.

This is what happened to the Bin Ladens in the years I lived with them, and it's what happened to Saudi Arabia as a whole while I was there. It is still happening today.

Meanwhile, I was beginning to make real friendships, and that helped. Salem's younger brother Bakr had moved into Salem's former house, just across the road from our own. Bakr himself was rather aloof—polite and pleasant, but always heavily aware of his high rank in the Bin Laden family. I knew Yeslam didn't like him much. But Bakr's wife, Haïfa, was a delightful, bubbly woman, a blond, blue-eyed Syrian with (at the time) two sons.

Haïfa and I shared a sense of humor, and her two young sons were a few years older than Wafah. She and Bakr had lived in Miami for a while; she spoke English, and understood my claustrophobia. But she had moved to Saudi Arabia years before me, and because of her Arab background she melded into the Bin Laden family far more deftly than I ever could.

Haïfa was different from me, but she was a kind of ally— my Arab counterpart. She was open-minded, and lively, and friendly, and I was grateful for that. Haïfa was also a gifted

mimic. She imitated to perfection one mother-in-law's wad-
dle and my own lopsided gait, with high heels and handbag
under a half-askew abaya. She was fun.

I think that I was a relief for Haïfa, too. Coming from
the freer atmosphere of Syria, she struggled with the strict
monotony of Saudi Arabia, as I did. Safe in Haïfa's garden,
tanning by her swimming pool, we howled with laughter at
how depraved the mothers-in-law would think us if they
caught sight of our bathing suits. We paddled together with
our children. And it was Haïfa who taught me, much more
even than Yeslam, about the etiquette I should follow and
the various marriages and funerals and events I must, as a
Bin Laden wife, attend.

The first time I took the decision to walk to her house
across the street—the first time I turned up at Haïfa's house
on foot, having crossed the few meters of road *by myself*, instead of calling for my driver—Haïfa grinned wildly. "Carmen!" she cried. "The revolution! Tomorrow all the Bin
Ladens will be saying, 'We saw Carmen *on the street*!'"

Haïfa loved her husband. It was not a completely
arranged marriage: They had met in Syria, and there was af-
fection between them—something I rarely perceived in Bin
Laden couples. In 1978, Haïfa gave birth to her third child,
a girl. I went to congratulate her a day later, just as Bakr arrived with their two sons. He told them, "Kiss your mother's
hand. She has given you a little sister." It was formal, but it
was sweet. It showed respect, I thought. There was real love
in that marriage—it was one of the few marriages I saw in
Saudi Arabia where that was true.

I became pregnant again. I was overjoyed, and I felt that

Yeslam was as well. A companion for Wafah—another baby—and surely this time we would have a boy. The whole Bin Laden clan seemed so happy to hear our news: I was greeted everywhere with cries of "Insh'allah you will have a boy!" The baby was due in June 1977, and I flew to Geneva a couple of months before my due date, to be sure I was properly cared for.

The Bin Laden family had the right to use the special royal family suites in all the best Saudi hospitals, but I didn't really trust the doctors there. Most of them were trained in Syria and Egypt, and they seemed far too ready to pump you full of pills and injections. The other Bin Laden women usually gave birth in Jeddah, but for special checkups they often went abroad, to Europe or the United States. A large portion of our traveling time overseas was always taken up by medical visits.

My mother and sisters took care of me in my last few weeks of pregnancy. I rested in the mild spring sunlight, and watched Wafah playing in my mother's garden—just as I once had, so many years ago. I could tell Wafah felt at ease in my mother's home, and Yeslam visited us frequently. It was a gentle period, one I would often look back to in the hard years to come.

Longing for a boy was not just a whim that occupied me in those last weeks of pregnancy. For Saudi women, it is essential to produce male heirs. It is not just a question of your personal status in society (though for many women that is part of the issue—to be called Om Ali, for example, sounds a lot better than plain Om Sarah). It can be a question of basic survival.

In the event of a husband's death, if his wife has only daughters, then the wife and girl children—even if they are adult—become dependent on the husband's closest male relative. He is their guardian, and must approve even basic decisions, such as travel, or education, or the choice of a husband. Even in terms of inheritance, a family with only women is discriminated against. When the husband dies, if he leaves only daughters, then 50 percent of his inheritance reverts to his parents and siblings. The wife and children receive just half his estate.

Only if the wife has sons does the entire estate pass to her and her children. And, once he is an adult, the oldest son can act as guardian to his mother and sisters.

Insh'allah, I would have a boy.

At last, my contractions began—a little ahead of schedule. Before heading for the clinic to give birth, I phoned Yeslam, who was still in Saudi Arabia. "Can't you wait till tomorrow, when my plane arrives?" he asked, in a rather petulant tone. I had to laugh at him—he was so used to having his way. Did he think I could delay a baby's birth to accommodate his schedule?

The baby was a girl, a beautiful little girl. She was perfect. I loved her instantly. We called her Najia, a name I always liked. It means the same thing as Yeslam—Protected.

Najia was a delight. She was the easiest baby a mother could wish for. She added so much to my life. She was so sweet and fragile. And now that I knew better what lay in store for her as a girl in Saudi Arabia, I did wish so much—for her sake—that she had been a boy.

I wondered sometimes, watching my children: If Yeslam had been a European man, would having two girls have been such an issue? Sensing my turmoil, Yeslam tried to comfort me. He insisted that it didn't matter; but something inside me told me differently. And I felt I had let him down.

I knew by now that in Saudi Arabia it was vital that I have a son. If I'd had a son, I would have brought him up to know that women are equal to men. He would have protected his sisters if anything happened to Yeslam. With a boy, even without Yeslam's help, we would have a close defender with values I could relate to.

At the time, of course, I could not know this, but in a sense it was Najia who, years later, would save us all. If I had had a boy, it would have been easier to cope with Saudi ways. We were wealthy, and respected; our lives were comfortable there. But because I had two little girls to care for, in the years to come I would become more sensitive to the dismal, oppressive conditioning that Saudi girl children must suffer as they grow into women. With little Najia and Wafah in my care, I ultimately found myself compelled to save my daughters from that culture. I simply could not watch my precious daughters submit.

So Najia was heaven-sent. Not only was she delightful, but she subsequently gave me the strength I would need to deliver us all from the influence of Saudi Arabia.

CHAPTER 9

Two Mothers, Two Babies

W E HEADED BACK TO SAUDI ARABIA THAT AUGUST. It was steaming hot, and a group of the Bin Laden brothers made plans for a day trip to the family country house in Taef, in the mountains, about two hours' drive from Jeddah. This was a vast house, built in the 1950s or 1960s, devoid of any special charm, but it was a little cooler there. It made for a change of routine. We women established ourselves in the female quarters, with the children.

My little Najia was a few months old, and Osama's wife, Najwah—a Syrian girl, the daughter of one of his mother's brothers—had a baby, Abdallah, who was about the same age. Osama's baby commenced howling, and kept it up for hours. He was thirsty. Najwah kept trying to feed him water with a teaspoon, but it was obvious this tiny baby was far too small to manage to drink properly from a spoon. My little Najia was gulping water from her baby bottle constantly, and I offered it to Najwah.

"Take it, he's thirsty," I told her.

But Najwah wouldn't take the bottle. She was almost crying herself. "He doesn't want the water," she kept saying. "He won't take the spoon."

Om Yeslam had to explain to me that Osama didn't want the baby to use a bottle. There was simply nothing Najwah could do about it. She was so sad, and so powerless—a drab little figure, very young, cradling her baby in the fold of her arm, watching him in such obvious distress. I couldn't stand it.

It was punishingly hot outside: perhaps a hundred degrees. A baby can dehydrate in a few hours at such temperatures. I couldn't believe someone would really let his tiny child suffer so much over some ridiculous dogmatic idea about a rubber teat. I couldn't just sit there and watch this happen.

Surely Yeslam could do something. I couldn't go over to the men's side of the house to appeal to him to intercede: As a sister-in-law I was not permitted to enter the men's quarters unveiled. But a sister, who had grown up unveiled with her brothers, could go there. I begged one of the sisters to get Yeslam.

When Yeslam arrived, I railed at him. "Go and tell your brother that his child is suffering," I said. "The baby needs a bottle. This has to stop."

But Yeslam came back shaking his head. He told me, "It's no use. This is Osama."

I just could not believe it. All the way back to Jeddah from Taef it haunted me. Osama could do as he wished with his wife and child: That was a given. His wife didn't dare disobey him: This was a given, too. Worse still, nobody would dare intercede. Even Yeslam seemed to agree that Osama's rule over his household should be absolute. The force and command I had once seen in Yeslam, and admired, seemed to be dissipating in the hot Arabian air.

As Yeslam drove back down the hills to Jeddah I sat in silence, veiled, my fists clenched, staring in silence at the empty world outside. I felt suffocated.

I'm sure Osama would not have wanted to lose his baby. It was not as if he didn't care about the child. But to him, the baby's suffering was less important than a principle that he probably imagined stemmed from some seventh-century verse in the Koran. And his family was simply awed by Osama's zeal, intimidated into silence. For them, as for most Saudis, you simply could not be too excessive about your religious beliefs.

That is when I realized just how powerless I had become. I saw myself in Najwah's place. Ever since Najia's birth, one crucial question had been nagging at me. With two baby daughters, what would become of me if Yeslam were no longer around? Every woman in Saudi Arabia has a guardian who must approve almost everything she does. If Yeslam were not there, and if I did not have a son to take on that role, my guardian—and the guardian of my daughters— would be one of Yeslam's brothers. I would be dependent for everything on that man.

Unless I had a son, I would need a brother-in-law's approval to leave the country, or even Jeddah. Wafah and Najia could be denied an education, or married to a person of their guardian's choosing, without any input from me. Men like Osama could one day rule over me and my children. There would be nothing whatsoever that I could do about it.

All that long drive back to town, I thought about the mothers I knew who were forced to live without their children. It was a litany of women who had no control over their lives—who had no recourse. There was Taiba, one of Yeslam's sisters, a tragic figure. Her husband had divorced her, and he had kept her two small daughters—they were aged four and seven when we first met. Taiba was permitted to see them only on Friday afternoons. Om Yeslam said the children cried bitterly every time Taiba had to leave them. Taiba was a sad, faded woman—old, somehow, and worn, though she must have been well under thirty.

One dear friend of mine had previously been married to a Saudi man, then divorced. She had planned to keep her two-year-old son with her: Although a man may choose to keep his children after he discards a wife, it is quite common to allow a small child to stay with his mother. But one afternoon, in Beirut, at the tailor's, my friend let go of her son's hand. A few minutes later, he was gone—kidnapped by his Saudi father. She never saw him again, though she begged for even one visit.

Najia, another of Yeslam's sisters, married her husband just before I arrived in Saudi Arabia. After he divorced her, she never saw her four children. I would implore her, "Why don't your brothers do something about it?" and Najia would just smile at me—"Ah, Carmen"—as if I were some kind of village idiot. You could never say an ill word about the brothers. And a husband's rule could not be questioned.

It ate at me. I felt a heavy weight inside. What if Yeslam had an accident right then, driving back to Jeddah? What if he were no longer there, to protect my small, now bitter-tasting, freedoms? What would be my daughters' destiny, as Saudi women? Who would decide their lives? Would it be Salem? Bakr? Ibrahim? And who could say what those men would become, with age and power? I would become a kind of beggar, completely dependent on their whims, as they controlled my children's lives in every minor detail.

For the first time, I felt a real gulf open between Yeslam and me, on a matter that counted more for me than any-thing else in the world. When I sought his reassurance—about a subject that was torturing me—he seemed dismissive. I needed him to take steps to find a way to resolve the problem—some kind of plan, a roadmap that could guide me in case of a tragedy, to make sure that I would al-ways be in charge of our girls, whatever life might have in store. I wanted him to tell me that he would always look after us—make sure we would always be safe from the whims of those men. To me, a man protects his family, thinks ahead, makes provision to keep them safe.

But somehow, it didn't concern him. Yeslam could not understand the depth of my fear. And when I finally grasped that, it made me even more afraid.

Suddenly, I felt I was alone. I was in need. And I was com-pletely powerless.

Nothing was ever the same after that day in Taef. My hopes for a freer world in the future, where women would at least be able to have a say in their children's lives, were for-ever shattered and buried in the Arabian desert sand by the dogmatic Wahabi perception of Islam. Emotionally, the fear and loneliness I felt then colored everything I was to see and live through in the years to come. Although I tried to behave as though everything was normal, a constant worried feeling now accompanied me everywhere. I was no longer a carefree mom. The future had a bitter taste to it now.

CHAPTER 10

My Own Chief Inmate

I TRIED TO PUT MY PANIC BEHIND ME. ALTHOUGH IT remained in the back of my mind as long as I lived in Saudi Arabia, I had to get on with my life. I distracted myself with a longed-for new project. Om Yeslam and Fawzia had decided to move out, and Yeslam had given them a parcel of land adjoining ours for their own house. Now that Yeslam and I had two little babies, we were a real family. And now I could try to make us all a real home, a home of our own.

I hired a cook—I had no desire to work in my kitchen as Om Yeslam did—and laid out plans to knock down walls and open out our gloomy, ill-planned rooms. I designed a new kitchen adjoining the house, big panels of sliding glass to open out the living room, and new quarters for the two female servants.

By this time, I had begun speaking directly to our male servants—the houseboy, the cook, the gardener, the doorman, and our two drivers. They lived in a separate lodging beside the gate. One afternoon I found the intercom wasn't functioning, and went out to their quarters to call Abdou, my driver. Poking my head around the door, I found a scene of such squalor that I could not help investigating further. As the servants were watching a football match at Bakr's servants' quarters, I asked Abdou to stand at the door and make sure no one followed me. I couldn't risk being found alone with one of the male servants in their bedroom. As I rapidly inspected their quarters, I discovered a kitchen that was unbelievably dirty, and smelled foul; the walls were black with grime. Even the bedrooms were filthy.

It was my own property, but I felt almost as if I was trespassing. No woman had ever been inside that lodging. The men who lived there went home to see their wives and families perhaps once every two years. They scorned what they considered women's work, and though they had to clean my home, they lived in their own rooms almost like animals. I was horrified by what I had stumbled upon, inside the walls of my own compound. I made Abdou buy paint, and gave the men money for new furniture; I insisted that they clean up.

Meanwhile, I got on with redecorating our house. It was a relief; but I had not foreseen the extent of the challenge. Shopping for furnishings was almost impossible: There were no shops. Finally I discovered that one Lebanese woman married to a Saudi had set up a kind of furniture store on the first floor of her villa, with modern furniture she purchased in Europe on trips abroad. It was an odd sort of shop—half home, half warehouse—but I did at least manage to pick out new, thick, cream carpeting. The nasty dark green wall-to-wall had to go.

How to carpet the house, though? Because I could not be seen or spoken to by the male workers, I had to assume that they knew their craft, and rely on Yeslam's Egyptian male secretary to direct the team. I resigned myself to this obvious waste of his time and energy, briefed him, and when the team of workers arrived, I agreed to retreat to a back room for the entire day. It was dusty, it was noisy, and the children were tetchy—and that evening, when I emerged, my eyes met a shambles. The carpeting had been laid at right angles to our big new windows, so that every seam was clearly visible. It looked no better than the shoddy old green one.

I told Yeslam the work would have to be redone; he sighed, and next morning instructed the workers to tear it up and replace it. Next day, we returned to our cloister. Next night, the carpet seams were less obvious, but a flawed piece had been laid right in the middle of the floor, exactly where it would be most visible. I certainly didn't want to live for years with this obvious mistake. So I told Yeslam it would have to be redone again.

I'm not sure Yeslam even knew what I was talking about. Certainly he was frustrated: He had plenty of better things to do, and having lived in the West he found the whole ring-around almost as tiresome as I did. So next morning he just said, "Go. Tell them yourself."

This was truly a gigantic step. For a Bin Laden woman to talk to a male worker—an outsider, not even a household servant, practically a stranger from the street—was unheard of. I cloaked my body and hair in my abaya, but kept my face free of the impenetrable black gauze face veil—I needed to see properly. And then I emerged from my back room to see the workers, and tell them what to do.

They would not look at me. I told them to tear out the carpeting again. They would not listen to me. The Sudanese worker who was laying down more carpeting simply laid down some more. I repeated myself. I raised my voice. Finally he turned his head slightly, still not facing me. "I do not take orders from women," he growled.

Only when Yeslam's secretary arrived, and insisted repeatedly that I was in charge of the work and he should listen to what I said, did the, by now, soiled and tiresome carpeting finally get laid. Later, in my bedroom, I boiled with frustration. I didn't know whether to laugh or cry. Every single gesture I could make in this world seemed to be under the control of a man. I had never in my life felt so dependent.

But I soothed myself: Life was changing. There was building all around us now. When I first arrived, the Bin Laden houses at Kilometer Seven were completely isolated; the desert was just behind my garden. Now, Jeddah had become a colossal building site that stretched toward us down the Mecca Road. Donkey Square and its squalid, dark grocery stores was being transformed into Dome Square, with a huge, modern public space that was quite beautiful. Every time I returned from a stay of a few weeks in Geneva, I found I couldn't recognize new parts of the city.

So in a physical sense, Saudi Arabia had changed—had changed immensely. Nowhere on the planet has anywhere developed as suddenly as Saudi Arabia did in the first five or six years that I lived there. Half a century before, people had wrapped themselves in wet sheets at night to get cool enough to sleep; now everyone seemed to have air-conditioning. There were car dealerships everywhere: At some, you could even bring in camels to use as part trade-in for a new Toyota.

Awash with petrodollars, it seemed that the Saudis could not spend enough.

The first fashion boutiques were sprouting up—staffed only by women, so you could remove your face veil to look at the clothes, or even disrobe to try items on. Women indulged in shopping frenzies. Underneath their veils, the younger women were made up like movie stars now, dressed in the latest European designs.

Hairdressers still came to the house: Hair was a major preoccupation, hidden away, then erotically displayed only to husbands. We women continued to live in almost complete seclusion from the world of men. But stores brimmed now with the accessories of the modern world—electronic gadgets and expensive sneakers. And suddenly a Safeway supermarket leapt into being downtown.

It became the height of excitement to go shopping at Safeway. I was the only Bin Laden woman who dared go out alone with my driver, though: The others always took friends, or at least a maid, along. It was a social occasion. From time to time you might even see husband and wife shopping together. Now every modern product could be bought—and it was. We filled basket after basket with Jell-O and Campbell's Soup, Swiss cheese and chocolate. Bread from the bakery still came peppered with weevils—I insisted my cook learn to bake bread—but now we had pineapple chunks and real milk. They tasted of progress.

By now I was used to my abaya and its cumbersome folds, but it still occasionally betrayed me. One day I was shopping, accompanied by my driver, Abdou, when I tripped over the black cloth. I tumbled down the stairs and somehow managed to roll myself up in the folds of it; I was trapped, like a mummy, completely unable to get up. I raised my head slightly; I could see Abdou, smiling in embarrassment. He didn't dare approach to help me up. I laughed, too—I couldn't help but see the comedy of the situation—and clumsily made it back on my feet without his help.

The fever of consumerism infected even the staid Bin Laden women. Safeway was just the beginning; now, too, my sisters-in-law began redecorating. But the furnishings they chose were loud and garish, terrible imitations of the objects I had carefully chosen. In Fawzia's house, everything was bright and shiny and mismatched. She kept the plastic flowers. You could see the plumbing pipes in the bathroom; the workmanship was shoddy. Fawzia and the others never complimented me on the house I had worked to build, because they didn't think I was worthy of their admiration. They copied me, and yet they lorded it over me. It always came down to one thing: They were Saudis. I was not.

I read voraciously—I was developing quite a library. I brought back crateloads of books from Geneva: the dreaded customs officials were not bold enough to search Bin Laden luggage for literary contraband. I read politics, economics, biographies, philosophy—anything challenging that I could lay my hands on. One time I read a magazine article about female circumcision—the horrible practice of mutilating girls' genitals, which is still common in Egypt and parts of West Africa.

Om Yeslam was in the kitchen, and I was so upset by what I had read that I blurted it out to her. I suppose I wanted comfort. I certainly didn't expect the reaction I received. She smiled at me and said, "It's not so bad, you know. An Egyptian woman comes, and it is just a little cut, such a little cut. The girl is very young. It doesn't hurt so very much."

Was Om Yeslam among the women who had been so barbarically mutilated? Was Fawzia? Was Sheikh Mohamed's eldest daughter, Aïsha? How many of the family's wives and daughters carried this awful emotional and physical scar among all their other secrets? Was there no end to the pain that Saudi women had to bear? I ran to my babies, and held them for a long time. My perfect little girls.

SLOWLY, AS WE BEGAN CIRCULATING A LITTLE MORE, I began to feel the beginnings of social progress. Younger, more modern-thinking Saudis began to relax their observance of traditions. A few women—then more and more—began to discard the opaque black face veil. They walked through shopping malls (though rarely on the public streets) with the bare triangles of their faces exposed, although everyone still had to wear the abaya over her hair and body. Om Yeslam herself began keeping her face veil off in front of her driver. She even began to speak to him directly.

I, meanwhile, vowed that I would be myself inside my own house. Life outside was far from normal, but I would run my household my way. It would be a refuge: my haven.

I saw the servants as people, like myself, but in different circumstances, and I sought to understand them. I know that the servants liked me: I was polite, and didn't bark orders like the other women; my children said please and thank you. Though I may have been demanding, I was never insulting. This was unusual, and widely remarked. The Bin Ladens saw them as objects—they functioned adequately, or they were stupid.

One time, after a sandstorm, I asked our elderly Pakistani doorman to clean the marble terrace we had installed outside the house. He took the new mop I had purchased, wet it, and began moving it around in circles. The result was muddy circles. I repeated my request; the result was the same. I admit I raised my voice—I was exasperated. I asked him what, exactly, he could not understand about this simple task. But then I stopped myself. What did this poor man know of mopping? He had lived most of his life with a beaten-earth floor. So I kicked off my sneakers, hiked up the legs of my pants, and began to show him how to mop, in straight lines.

Yeslam arrived just at that moment. "*What* are you doing?" he cried at me, infuriated. I hurried inside. I didn't know what he thought was worse—displaying my ankles to a man, or mopping the floor. A Bin Laden woman does neither.

I found that incident rather amusing; but on other occasions I was somewhat less forgiving. I once found Yeslam's Yemeni driver parked inside our compound, in front of our house, with the motor running. Even from a distance of a few meters I could feel the heat coming off the engine and could smell it burning. I said, "Turn off the engine, it's going to overheat." But Yeslam's driver ignored me. "I have to keep the air-conditioning on for Sheikh Yeslam," he said. When I insisted, he added, "I don't take orders from women."

It was so insulting and absurd—the car was on the verge of bursting into flames! I yelled at him, "When Sheikh Yeslam is not here, I'm the one in charge!" Bakr heard the commotion from his house across the street, and came over to intervene. Needless to say, the driver immediately turned off the engine.

Life went on. We put in a tennis court. I so longed for exercise. Yeslam had learned to play in Los Angeles, and I ordered dozens of rackets and shoes in every size: We began inviting people for tennis parties on Thursday nights.

This was another attempt to create a normal life. I would wear normal clothes; we would serve barbecued sirloin steaks and beer, just like in America. It was a little tricky to buy alcohol on the black market—it is banned in Saudi Arabia. But embassy personnel brought it in under diplomatic seal, and the drivers ran an underground commerce. One of our employees purchased beer from the chauffeurs of an African consulate. We were safe: The religious police never dared to inspect the homes of princes—or Bin Ladens.

I was the only woman in the family who received men at home. Haïfa used to say, "At least Yeslam comes home. He spends time with you. He talks with you. He lets you live your life." Haïfa wasn't jealous. She was glad for me, pointing out ways in which Yeslam was special. She didn't want to brave the world in the same way that I seemed to need. She was trying to help me adjust to my Saudi life—to be happy.

My Thursday night parties did preserve my sanity, I think. Foreigners would come—diplomats, Western businessmen, and a few Arabs working for multinational corporations, who had headed for the booming Gulf only to be crippled by their social isolation. The visiting businessmen, in particular, were infinitely grateful for a break from the dismal hotel rooms where they often waited for weeks to be received by some prince or arrogant local businessman. Dealing with Saudi Arabia was so difficult for them: the endless waiting, the inactivity, all the restrictions.

Many expatriates living in Saudi Arabia were so desperate for amusement and escape, they brewed their own moonshine alcohol in their bathtubs. Once, at Safeway, I saw a huge crowd of expats, all gathered around a display of chocolates, excitedly shoving dozens of boxes into each of their baskets. Curious about what was going on, I examined one man's purchases in the checkout line. They were liqueur chocolates, with Kirsch! I had a good laugh at that. Some customs official had obviously slipped up.

Our Thursdays were open house—anything from twenty-five to seventy people. There were regulars, like the American ambassador, John West, and his wife, Lois, friends who have stood by me to this day. Their daughter, Shelton, was about twenty years old. I could barely imagine how difficult Saudi life must have been for her, a young, single American girl in such a closed society.

In contrast, the atmosphere at our house was really relaxed, like the social events I'd so enjoyed in America. We set up a TV room for the children, with videos. People brought their friends. For the expats, these evenings became a real event on what passed for the Jeddah social calendar. The first time the wife of the Belgian ambassador came, she was resplendent in an elaborate long dress, and visibly startled to see me in Capri pants, alongside men wearing shorts. "Wow, it really *is* casual!" she exclaimed. "Every time somebody says 'casual' in this country I find everyone dressed to a T. This is so unexpected!"

The tennis was a distraction; it relaxed the atmosphere. Most of us talked. People came with the latest news; we talked about politics, or books. (My much envied bookshelves were becoming a kind of community library.) Other times, the businessmen would talk about major contracts they were negotiating, and the expanding opportunities in the country.

These were the people who were building the new, modern Saudi Arabia. Talking with them—listening to them and having them listen back—became my lifeline. It was stimulating, a challenge. And the socializing was also good for Yeslam's business. When these men, often directors of major corporations, came to Yeslam's home to play tennis, eat, and drink a beer, it opened new doors for Yeslam. It made him different from other Saudis. It was quite something to be invited to Yeslam's house.

Yeslam was becoming influential. He was from the great Bin Laden family. And even within the hierarchy of Bin Laden brothers, Yeslam was rising to become a major player, someone to be reckoned with.

Sometimes Yeslam would invite Saudi men to these

tennis parties, but no Saudi woman ever came. I felt defiant about maintaining normality when Saudi men were around. I thought that if the men saw me speaking freely with Yeslam they would get used to it, and maybe realize how much richer and more worthwhile it was to have a relationship of exchange and companionship with your wife. I thought I was helping Saudi society evolve. But perhaps most Saudis found the casual atmosphere too threatening to handle. Though Yeslam's brothers often dropped in, they never stayed.

One Thursday evening in 1978 all the diplomats were talking about the latest rumor that was racing through Jeddah. One of the King's young great-nieces, Princess Mish'al, had been cold-bloodedly murdered in a parking lot downtown. Barely an adult, Mish'al had been promised in marriage to a much older man. She had tried to flee the country with her lover, using another passport. She had been captured at the airport.

No woman can leave Saudi Arabia—or even travel outside the city she lives in—without the written permission of her husband or father, or son. A woman is never a legal adult. But there exists a women's underground network that trades passports and permissions. Because no customs official would dare ask a woman to unveil, it is not difficult to assume another identity.

Nonetheless, Mish'al had been caught. I don't know how. And her grandfather, Prince Mohamed, the brother of King Khaled, had ordered her killed, for bringing shame on her family. King Khaled had apparently resisted his brother's order, but Prince Mohamed had insisted that she be killed, and he was the patriarch of his clan. There was no trial, I was told. Mish'al was shot six times in a parking lot downtown. A British man passing by had taken photos. Now, to the Saudi government's fury, the BBC was planning to air a documentary.

I was rigid with horror. I thought about it for a long time. A grandfather could order his young granddaughter put to death because she had fallen in love; and nobody could prevent it.

This was not even an Islamic issue. In some sense, it went deeper than that. There had been no trial by an Islamic court; no edict from the imams. The force at work in this dramatic, awful event was the old Bedouin culture of Saudi Arabia—savage, bitter customs that maintain their grip on society to this day.

In Bedouin culture, clan loyalty is all you can count on. As nomads, Bedouins travel light: The family is the anchor of the tribe. Women and camels are a Bedouin tribe's only possessions. Ruthlessness is a positive value in the desert. And honor, for reasons I cannot even begin to fathom, does not come from compassion, or good works—it is focused on the absolute possession of women. Women are not free in any way—not even free to have emotions, such as love, or longing. A disobedient woman dishonors her clan and is eliminated.

My first thought when I heard about Mish'al was for my innocent little girls. This could happen one day to Wafah or Najia. One of their uncles might be perfectly capable of ordering his niece put to death. And I would be powerless. There are no words to describe my anger and my renewed panic that day. If our family trip to Taef had been my first wake-up call to the reality of Saudi Arabia, Mish'al's death was surely the second.

I DECIDED TO CELEBRATE THE JOINT BIRTHDAYS OF Wafah and Najia in May. I had no idea how many religious quandaries would be raised by this simple and innocent decision. I just went ahead and phoned all the sisters-in-law to invite their children. My sister-in-law Rafah was particularly startled.

"We don't even mark the birthday of the Prophet Mohamed," Rafah insisted. "Christians mark birthdays. Christmas is a birthday."

"What are you saying?" I replied, bewildered. "This isn't some kind of idol worship. I just want to show a little girl that I'm happy she was born. I'm saying, 'You were born that day, for me it was a happy day.' It isn't Christian."

I didn't convince her. For Rafah and the others, it was a matter of religion. And they were steadfast. In Saudi Arabia—for Bin Ladens—I learned that birthday celebrations are *haram.*

It may have been a trivial issue, but it really annoyed me. Rafah and the others were convinced they held the deeper truth. They saw the West as depraved, a decadent culture on the verge of collapse. It became important to me—perhaps excessively so. I didn't want to renounce everything about my culture to please the Bin Ladens. I was not going to deprive my children of something so basic as a birthday. Yeslam agreed to let me do it. It was not the first time we had braved tradition.

I decided to mark the day with another project: huge cutout polystyrene figures that I would make with scissors and pins. They would be much more beautiful than store-bought decorations, and they would show my girls that not everything must be bought from a shop. I worked for weeks. Perhaps out of curiosity, several of the sisters-in-law came, along with their children. They played and shrieked till late. It was like a fairy-tale celebration.

But every year, as the children grew older, it got harder to persuade their mothers to permit them to attend. Despite my friendship with Haïfa, I still felt alone. I was living in a society where women were nothing and wanted to be nothing. They didn't seem to seek the changes that I was expecting and longing for, and I felt frustrated, surrounded by women who didn't have the will or courage to resist. They had intelligence and energy, many of them, but they expressed it only in religion. They lived, but only for their faith; their personalities were completely annihilated.

I was mistress of my own house now, but there were days when I also felt like its chief inmate. After the evening prayer call, at dusk, I would stand on the marble terrace we had installed, and listen to the thousands of birds that wheeled overhead, calling to each other as the huge, orange sun sank into the desert behind our house. They made an incredible racket, wheeling across the desert in black clouds, and there was almost nothing else to see for miles. It was beautiful, but it was always, always the same—stark, empty of imagination, creativity, and real companionship.

As the months went by, I found these silent vigils gave me a heavy, claustrophobic feeling. My baby girls were inside the house, behind me; but my life sometimes felt as barren and empty as the sand.

CHAPTER 11

The Brothers

AS BEFIT HIS RANK AS THE TENTH SON OF SHEIKH Mohamed, Yeslam occupied a rather junior position in the Bin Laden Organization during our first year in Saudi Arabia. To my delight, though, it soon became obvious to all that his talents were being wasted. Yeslam was far more intelligent and better educated than his brothers. And the Bin Laden Organization wasn't doing as well as it appeared. The company badly needed Yeslam's skills.

At the time, the Bin Laden Organization was still being run by a board of eight trustees, who had been appointed by King Faisal after Sheikh Mohamed died, to look after the interests of Mohamed's young children. (When he died, at the age of fifty-nine, only two of Sheikh Mohamed's sons had reached the age of twenty-one.) The company was among the largest in Saudi Arabia, and as such deserved special care. Moreover, Sheikh Mohamed had worked for King Faisal's father, the fabled Abdel Aziz, and his brother, King Saud, building most of their palaces and helping out in other ways. He had a bond with the royal family.

The eight trustees, all fine, respectable older men, were nonetheless deeply conservative and completely averse to taking risks. Other construction companies had begun growing alongside the stagnating Bin Laden Organization, some of them sponsored by powerful princes. It was said that these competitors were better connected than the Bin Ladens; and in Saudi Arabia, connections are your bottom line. The Bin Laden Organization's competitors were aggressive and powerful. They were winning contracts left and right.

Meanwhile, there was also trouble among the brothers. Salem was Sheikh Mohamed's oldest son; his second son, by another wife, was named Ali. (I had met him in Lebanon.) When Sheikh Mohamed sent Salem away to be educated abroad, he decided to keep Ali in Saudi Arabia. When Sheikh Mohamed died, both Salem and Ali were legally adults, and Salem decided to take his rightful place as ruling male in the family and the corporation. Ali, who came second, but who had stayed at his father's side, felt that he should be in charge.

For years Ali contested Salem's decisions, and the rivalry between the brothers was doing the company no good. Finally, Ali petitioned King Faisal for permission to leave the Bin Laden Organization, and Saudi Arabia. Although Ali's claim to be Sheikh Mohamed's true successor did have some merit, the King had to agree to his departure from the company. Even King Faisal could not permit the rule of the oldest brother to be contested. It is the foundation of the clan system of Saudi Arabia—the foundation of the royal family itself.

So Ali received permission to break away from the Bin

Laden Organization, and his family. The Bin Ladens and the trustees estimated the value of the company—something they had not previously done, since the children and their mothers had planned to share it—and gave Ali $1 million. He left for Lebanon. Salem, and his younger brother Bakr, took over.

The Bin Laden Organization still had the prestigious and lucrative exclusive contract to renovate Mecca and Medina, but the company was flagging elsewhere. Yeslam began to rise through the ranks. He hired two men from Citibank and began restructuring the main Jeddah office. Yeslam created departments, and formal reporting and decision-making processes, where once there had been consensus, and endless delay. Yeslam was the first to bring in computers, and little by little he took over the company's finances, negotiating loans and investments with major foreign banking conglomerates. He began joint ventures with companies like General Motors and Losinger, a Swiss construction company.

The Bin Laden Organization was jointly owned by Sheikh Mohamed's heirs, in a complex arrangement. The four wives who were still formally married to him when he died shared one eighth of their inheritance among themselves. The remaining seven eighths of the company went to his fifty-four children: a full share to the sons, half as much to the daughters. (Since a discarded wife did not directly inherit, her children supported her as a matter of course.) The company was operated in common—not even a parcel of land could be bought or sold without full agreement—and none of the brothers, at the time, received a salary. Every child took a dividend every year—one share for boys, half a share for girls. In reality, however, it was the oldest brother, Salem, and his ally, Bakr, who ran the show.

Salem and Bakr had the same mother. Officially, there are no half-brothers in a Saudi family, but still there were affinities, groupings—whether because the men shared the same mother, or because they were the same age, or had gone to the same schools. If they had all three factors in common, as Salem and Bakr did, the tie was even closer.

Yeslam's natural allies were all younger than him. And like many of the younger men, he chafed under his older brothers' rule.

One evening, when everything was closed, Yeslam took me to see the offices, carefully shrouded, of course, in my abaya. The building was near Kilometer Seven and it looked like—like nothing. It bore no resemblance to a major Western corporation, all glass and power. I saw long corridors, like an old provincial high school in Europe, with bare little rooms. A man was sweeping—just sweeping, not even using a vacuum cleaner—so I had to retreat into Yeslam's office. It was simple: a wood table, no carpets, and just three cheaply framed pictures on the wall, of King Abdel Aziz, King Faisal, and King Khaled. It looked nothing like the head office of one of the most important companies in the Middle East.

The other brothers soon realized that Yeslam's skills were vital. His star began rising. Yeslam's place was at the Jeddah headquarters of the business now. He was consulted. He knew about finance, and about the West. But some of his older brothers didn't welcome Yeslam's growing stature: His reputation was starting to overshadow their own.

To maintain his position, Yeslam badly needed powerful friends. Hassan was a very capable older brother who had no natural allies, since his mother had had only one son. Hassan became Yeslam's ally, even though Yeslam came just tenth in rank and Hassan was fifth.

The lines of allegiance were constantly shifting, according to unspoken disputes and private agendas. If Omar wanted to buy a piece of land, he might temporarily join with Yeslam's camp, say. This was a corporation, and like any corporation it was rife with internal politics. But it was also a family—and a carefully polished family, where no strife could ever be openly acknowledged.

The atmosphere of tension and secrecy was often stifling, and it began to weigh on Yeslam's spirits. He turned to me increasingly, for support and reassurance, to cope with the pressure he was under from his brothers. He needed a sounding board. I had become his strength. I found I was becoming a strategic counselor, an analyst, with a hoard of secret knowledge of the day-to-day goings-on behind the scenes at Yeslam's business. It was a role I welcomed: It kept my mind functioning, and it helped me feel involved in building a future for our family.

Yeslam was by now in effect the chief financial officer of the company. Many of the younger brothers began coming more often to our house in the evening, to drink tea on our terrace or have dinner, and talk. I would stay to eat with them, and listen, and since Yeslam did not order me away, they accepted my silent presence. Perhaps they did not realize that I knew enough Arabic to understand. The most religious among the brothers—Osama and others—rarely visited at such times, because I kept my face unveiled. If they did come, I had to retire to my room.

I learned to keep my own counsel. If I spoke, the brothers would go silent, and Yeslam would glare at me over his tea glass. I learned to stay still, and absorb knowledge. Many issues were not clearly stated, but I could divine the intended message. Later I might talk with Yeslam about what I had learned.

Sitting on my terrace sipping tea, this coterie of younger brothers would discuss business: decisions they planned to make, or counterorders that Salem and Bakr had issued. Many of them were frustrated by their lack of contact with the princes of the al-Saud family, who ruled the country with total power.

Cultivating a relationship with a benevolent, powerful prince could cost you much time, in lobbying, and also money. It involved paying court to him virtually every evening, traveling with him—and some of the al-Sauds skimmed a huge percentage off every major contract as their divine birthright. But the princes were also the gateways to success, prestige, and clout.

I didn't want Yeslam to remain the tenth in rank, a clever cog in a machine that was much larger than he was. I knew that he was brilliant, effectively skilled—he deserved more than that. But to become his own man—more than just another Bin Laden—Yeslam would need his own contacts with the al-Sauds. And Salem and Bakr guarded their contacts with the princes. These were doors on which you could not simply knock.

As our social life expanded, thanks to our Thursday night parties, we were meeting many more people. Many of them were foreigners who were only just discovering the extent of their isolation from the Saudis and from their own Western way of life. My friend Ula Sabag, a Swedish woman, was married to a Palestinian-American who had lived in Saudi Arabia for thirty years. Her husband, Issa, was a soft-spoken older man who worked as a translator and counselor at the U.S. embassy, and he was well placed in the entourage of Prince Majid, a portly, pasty-white figure who was one of the King's many brothers. (There had been twenty wives in that branch alone of the royal family.)

Like all the major al-Saud princes, Prince Majid received people every evening at his *majlis*, in a vast, regal room in his palace. It was a kind of court of supplicants, after the evening prayer. If they were not well known to him personally, Prince Majid would simply greet the visitors, and they would take their place on some distant settee. Close associates would be seated beside the Prince. That was the nexus of power.

Well-connected people might attend several such princely courts, as Salem did. He had several close sponsors, among them Prince Salman, the governor of Riyadh, and attended a different *majlis* virtually every night. One evening, Issa took Yeslam to meet Prince Majid.

Nothing special transpired that night—a little conversation, some cups of tea. Things go slowly in Saudi Arabia, in symbolic steps so infinitesimal that an outsider might not even notice. But soon a pattern was set. Yeslam became close to Prince Majid, then to other princes, too. Yeslam was becoming one of the men who sat close to power. He was talking, now, to other men who sat close to power as well. It was a subtle play of influence and gestures that had enormous impact on Yeslam's stature.

Later on, when Issa Sabag retired, he came to see us. He had lost his own position with the princes, but he had some administrative request, and asked Yeslam to take him along as part of his entourage. Yeslam agreed, but day after day he would avoid the old man before heading out to see the Prince. One day I cornered him and said, "Issa helped you when you needed him." But Yeslam dismissed me imperiously. "Nobody helped me," he said. "I am a Bin Laden."

But that was many years later. As Yeslam began consolidating his power within the Bin Laden Organization, the discussions on my terrace became more heated. Yeslam was now in effect running the company. But although they were earning big new contracts, Yeslam's rise was not welcomed by Salem and Bakr. One morning Bakr called a major bank to discuss a loan—some hundreds of millions of riyals—for a new building project. The banker foolishly asked, "Does Sheikh Yeslam know about this?" Bakr felt slighted. He had lost face.

Salem and Bakr began issuing counterorders to Yeslam's decisions. They claimed credit for his projects, and undercut and criticized his key employees. They turned down at the last minute agreements he had negotiated, embarrassing him. Then Hassan, who was a good businessman but lost a fortune at a London casino, phoned for help. Salem and Bakr paid Hassan's debts, but when he returned to Saudi Arabia, Yeslam found him detached. Hassan had switched camps.

Yeslam organized a major new contract to build the Bin Laden Plaza in downtown Jeddah. It was a spectacular skyscraper, in those days by far the tallest building in town, which cost hundreds of millions of dollars to construct. We made a lot of trips to Paris during those months: It was Yeslam who negotiated the contract and signed the agreements. We spent weeks at the plush George V hotel; I remember sitting on the bed, cross-legged, reading the contracts late into the night.

For the Bin Laden Organization, it was a fantastic financial coup—the first in a series. The entire project was financed by French bank loans, and guaranteed by the French government. All the Bin Laden Organization did was put up the land. When the entire building was rented to Saudia, the national airline, the French quickly recouped their investment. And the Bin Laden Organization subsequently made a fortune as the owners of, essentially, a free building.

Of course this could never have happened in any other country, because the French would simply have bought the land. But in Saudi Arabia foreigners may not own property. They may not even practice business without a Saudi partner. The sacred soil cannot be sullied by unbelievers.

I was so proud of what Yeslam had achieved in setting up the project. But when it was reported in the Saudi papers, they gave all the credit for Yeslam's work to smug Bakr.

I could see that it gnawed at Yeslam, but he would always back off at such times. He never confronted Bakr and Salem with what they were doing, although his private dislike of them grew even more vehement. He complained to me about his brothers' double-dealing, but he never took action to defend himself.

Confrontation is not a Saudi habit. On the surface, everything is calm—particularly within the clan. There is greed. There are struggles for power and honor—even among the royal family. The hidden daily reality is brother against brother, for even in Saudi Arabia, human nature pushes individuals to affirm their personality and ambition.

But in a deeper sense, their shared social conditioning and Wahabi convictions mean that members of a Saudi clan will always support one another. No individual destiny is more important than those shared religious values. For a Saudi, there can be no escape from the traditions of his ancestors.

CHAPTER 12

1979

CHANGE HAD COME TO SAUDI ARABIA, I REFLECTED on New Year's Day of 1979. My three years there had seen a gleaming new city rise out of the sandy dirt roads of medieval old Jeddah. Modern amenities were coming: No longer did the Bin Laden truck bring water to fill our cistern every two or three days. My girls were happy. I had Haïfa for comfort and fun. Yeslam adored me, and his scope and power were growing. Some young women even risked walking in the malls with their faces uncovered. I had everything to look forward to.

How could I possibly know how many steps backward the Middle East would swiftly take? In the coming months, a rebellion against the Shah in Iran would trigger a shock wave across the region and give a rush of new momentum to the traditionalists who fought against every attempt to bring the Middle East into the modern world. Islam would take on an entirely new dimension and change the outlook of the entire world. Nothing would ever be the same again.

Not even the lapdog Saudi newspapers could shield us

from the news that was flaming up in Iran. Revolution had broken out. In January, Shah Reza Pahlavi was forced to flee the country. A weird, awkward coalition of Western-influenced liberals and fanatical fundamentalists was calling for rule by the people. In February, Ayatollah Khomeini left his exile in France and arrived in Tehran, to be greeted by unbelievable crowds of millions of sympathizers. Then Khomeini's men began attacking the Westernized liberals who had helped them. They forced the veil on women who had previously chosen to walk the streets freely. Businesses were targeted for Islamic "reform." Everyone in the Middle East could feel the sudden, sinister wind of change.

At our Thursday evening parties, the diplomats and other foreigners could speak of nothing else. Everyone was insatiable for news. I was among the lucky ones: My sisters in Europe sent me newspapers and magazines weekly by DHL. I was overwhelmed by what was happening in Iran. My mother's homeland was being transformed by a revival of the Middle Ages. Acid was thrown in the faces of women who wore makeup. Thousands of people were arrested and killed. Khomeini criticized the Saudi monarchy. He said there could be no king in Islam.

I could see that the specter of revolution made Yeslam and his brothers nervous. I, too, watched anxiously. If the monarchy could be overturned in Iran—if free Iranian women could so swiftly be forced back into the chador, and suffer vicious attacks by the religious police on the street—then what could happen in Saudi Arabia?

I worried, too, about the people I knew in Iran. My mother was safe in Europe, though she seemed increasingly

In Jeddah, with Yeslam, my mother-in-law, Wafah, and Najia, in our garden

I had two babies now and we were a real little family. But the emotional loneliness I experienced after that terrible day at Taef had not left me.

Swimming with
Wafah in Haïfa's pool

Haïfa was a great friend to me. We kept in touch, even long after I left Saudi Arabia, but after 9/11 I never saw her again.

In December, with my mother and Yeslam in Geneva

We spent many Christmases in Geneva. It didn't seem to bother Yeslam that we marked such a Christian holiday, although later it became difficult for me to celebrate even my own children's birthdays.

A family Christmas, unpacking presents with the girls

With Yeslam and Najia, at our house in Jeddah

In public I wore the abaya, which covered my whole body. This photo of me partially uncovered may have been taken in our house, but as soon as I left the gate I would have had to adjust my abaya.

In Jeddah, Najia with some of the decorations that I made for the girls' birthday party

It was important to me that not everything in their lives came from a shop. I spent hours making those swans.

In our backyard

In Jeddah, my girls could only play within the confines of the house. And even there our lives were increasingly restricted. As Saudi culture began to regress, our small freedoms slipped away.

1981, Fawzia and Majid's wedding. Khalil, Salem, Yeslam, Om Yeslam, Fawzia, Majid, and his family

We pulled out all the stops for Fawzia's wedding. I was very fond of Majid and devastated when he was killed in a tragic accident just five years later.

Wafah and Najia at school in Jeddah

I was insistent that the girls should go to school, but worried by what they learned there.

By the poolside in Jeddah

Of course, photos are a very private matter in Saudi Arabia. But I was keen to have some pictures of my daughters growing up, so I asked the official photographer of the Bin Laden Organization to come to the house.

Wafah and Najia in Jeddah

In Jeddah on our last trip

As the girls grew up, Yeslam's behavior began to change. In a restrictive society he had allowed us small liberties, but in a free country, he became more and more closed.

Noor, who has never set foot in Saudi Arabia

At home in Geneva

This was the real beginning of freedom. Slowly, we all got used to living our lives without the constant fear of transgression.

After 9/11 our private lives became public and I felt that I had to let the world know where we stand.

Despite the year of struggle, my consolation is that I know now that my beautiful girls are free to be who they want to be.

frail. Most of her family had already emigrated, many of them settling in the United States. Still, my mother had countless friends and acquaintances living in Iran, and news of their living conditions was difficult to obtain and horrendous to imagine.

Deep down I still thought that if ever there were a revolution in Saudi Arabia I would be able to escape. As a foreigner, and as a Bin Laden, I knew I would be among the first to get out. That was the true luxury of my position, not the Chanel dresses and emerald earrings. We had the clout to get out if we had to—the power and status to escape the inspections of the religious police, get out of jail, or get out of the country.

The Bin Laden Organization had a fleet of airplanes. And if a Bin Laden wanted a seat on a plane, he could just take one. Because the Bin Laden Organization was the only company authorized to work in Mecca, the family's status was far higher than that of the other merchant clans. Even if an airplane was fully booked, Bin Ladens would always get a ticket. I had often seen this happen. In case of trouble, we could surely just fly ourselves out.

So although I was tense—you couldn't help but be—I didn't feel directly threatened. But the al-Saud princes who ran the country must have been much more frightened than I was. They had everything to lose. Khomeini's revolution was an outright attack on their rule. You could see the increasing influence of hard-line religious ideas on the street. The tiny changes that had given me so much hope for future freedom crumbled as the royal family panicked, and sought to placate the fundamentalists.

More extreme ideas of religious behavior took grip with a swiftness that stunned me. Notices were plastered in the souk warning about the dangers of improper dress. As sermons in the mosques began calling for more restrictions on social mores, more and more women began wearing the face veil again. Despite the punishing heat, they added thick black stockings under their abayas, to shield the few centimeters of feet and ankles that might be seen as they walked. Many, like Osama's wife, Najwah, and my sisters-in-law Rafah and Sheikha, started wearing gloves. The religious police—the mutawa—began wielding thick long sticks, like in Iran, to police our modesty, sometimes beating women in the street.

All of a sudden I began noticing little things, as if society was going backward. One afternoon, I was in a supermarket when a pregnant woman fainted; her husband rushed to help her up. The mutawa were there, and they stopped him, yelling at him that he must not take his wife in his arms in public.

If the prayer call rang out when we were shopping, we couldn't stay, as before, while the men went out to pray: The shopkeepers were frightened, and closed their shutters hurriedly.

The mutawa yelled at us in the street—"You, woman, what are you doing?"—if our hands were showing, or if my abaya was held too high. Abdou, my Sudanese driver, would always protect me—"Bin Laden." Even now, the religious integrity of a Bin Laden woman could not be questioned. Nonetheless, I began to be afraid.

The mutawa broke into homes and smashed hi-fis. If

they found alcohol, they hauled men off to jail and beat them there. They prohibited the sale of children's dolls— dolls became contraband, like whiskey, because they were human images. Suddenly, the only dolls for sale were shapeless figures with no faces, like the one owned by Aïsha, the Prophet Mohamed's child-wife, in the seventh century. But this was 1979!

There was no discussing such matters with the Bin Laden women. They would never have violated the rules in the first place. To them, the mutawa were doing their job, and that job was honorable and just. They felt certain there was no such thing as being too strictly religious. But the foreigners all noticed how much more severe, and terrifying, the mutawa had become.

Once I did strike up a conversation on the subject with my sister-in-law Rafah. We were talking about the veil, and I told her I found it unnecessary and insulting—insulting to Saudi men. Were they really so weak and so obsessed with sex that they would be tempted to sin by a mere glance at a woman's face? Rafah stared at me as though I'd been speaking ancient Greek. I could read it in her eyes— "poor ignorant foreigner." I simply could not get through to her.

It was the young people who frightened me most. They were supposed to lead the country forward, out of the Middle Ages, into the modern world. And yet I watched them week by week as they sped backward through the centuries. I saw their gloves and black stockings and their angry faces—heard the demands for more restrictions. Surely it could not be true that the young were in fact longing for the world to move into reverse? Who could believe such a thing? And yet it was happening in Iran.

I felt trapped. Every one of the changes I had welcomed seemed to have been temporary. Every little opening lasted so briefly. The Saudis had opened up to the world for a couple of years. Now, it seemed, they were retreating back to their values and traditions.

We went to the United States that summer. It was partly a business trip for Yeslam, but mostly I wanted to fold myself into Mary Martha's reassuring, loving embrace. She was glad to see me after the months of terrible upheaval; I felt such relief to be back in America again. But on the day before we were scheduled to leave Los Angeles for St. Louis, where Yeslam had meetings, Mary Martha phoned me, in tears. Her brother Jimmy had been lost flying his own plane between Arizona and California. A search was out, she told us, and she was flying to Arizona to be with her parents.

I couldn't leave Mary Martha at a time like that. I insisted that we stay with her. Yeslam went into overdrive. By the time Mary Martha and I reached Arizona, he had chartered two planes and was co-piloting one of them, searching for Jimmy. A whole fleet of planes stayed up in the air, dawn to dusk, till the wreckage of Jimmy's plane was found, five days later. Yeslam's face was tense and drawn. He didn't want to talk. It reminded me that his own father had been killed in a plane crash, when Yeslam was only seventeen.

My heart went out to Mary Martha, and to the Barkley family. But we had to go back, to Yeslam's business. We returned to Saudi Arabia, hearts heavy, words unspoken. It had been a dreadful summer.

ALL SAUDI ARABIA SEEMED MESMERIZED BY THE PO-litical volcano in Iran, and its fallout across the Middle East. It was all we talked about. One of our occasional guests, John Limbert, an American diplomat, played tennis with us one Thursday night in October, and told us he would be leaving for Iran the next day. Then, a few days later, he was taken hostage in the U.S. embassy in Tehran. He and dozens of others were paraded before the TV cameras to demonstrate the might of Islamic vengeance on the godless Americans. John was among the group of fifty-two hostages who were held in captivity for 444 days. Lois West tried to comfort his wife, Parvanai, through her terrible ordeal; we were all shaken.

Then one November morning Yeslam rushed home from work, ashen and agitated, and told me, "Mecca has been taken." Hundreds of Islamic extremists had stormed the Grand Mosque and seized control of Islam's holiest place. Through the muezzin, their leader was making incendiary statements about the corruption and loose living of some of the al-Sauds—particularly Prince Nayef, the governor of Mecca. The extremist forces had sneaked into Mecca using Bin Laden Organization trucks, which were never searched.

We must have been the first to know. The Bin Ladens kept a permanent staff of employees in a maintenance of-fice in Mecca. When the rebels stormed the Grand Mosque, a Bin Laden worker immediately phoned the head office in

Jeddah, and reported that violence had broken out. Then the insurgents cut the phone lines. Incredibly, it was the Bin Laden Organization that informed King Khaled that rebellion had broken out in Islam's holiest city.

One of the King's first decisions was to cut all phone lines in the nation. I wanted to phone my mother, to reassure her, but there was no way to get a line out. The newspapers didn't dare report the attack for several days. But the rumor spread anyway. There was tumult. Air traffic was grounded.

The house filled, then emptied, in a frenzy of movement as waves of brothers rushed in and out with the latest news. Yeslam was frantic, dashing from house to office like a man unhinged. The Bin Ladens had the only detailed maps of Mecca—the Grand Mosque in particular. Salem remained with the princes day and night. After days of discussion and attempts to negotiate with the extremists, they laid out plan after plan for military assaults on the extremist-held mosque. All of them failed.

Then Yeslam told me his brother Mahrouz had been arrested on the road driving from Mecca to Jeddah. The police had found a pistol in his car. Mahrouz was a very strictly religious man now, though he'd spent a few years in Lebanon enjoying a Western lifestyle. He wore his thobe short, to show his ankles and demonstrate his strict simplicity. Otherwise, though, I'd thought of him as just another of Yeslam's brothers. Had Mahrouz really been involved in a plot against the al-Sauds?

Finally, the famous French GIGN paratroopers were called in. They flooded the Mosque basement, killing many of the extremists. (They had to undergo the world's most rapid conversion to Islam before they could approach the building.) In a country with no journalism, rumors ran wild: The French had electrocuted the rebels; it hadn't been the French at all; the rebels hadn't really been captured. Then dozens of men were executed in public, across the country.

I knew there were many rumors that Mahrouz may have been involved, but he was released. People said he was the only suspect to have been freed from police custody. But the Bin Ladens never spoke again about his arrest. The Bin Laden family lived quietly, but they had the power to save their own.

Still, I no longer felt safe in my perfectly smooth gold-fish bowl. Nobody in Saudi Arabia slept well during those long, tense weeks.

In early December, we heard that violence had erupted in Qatif, in eastern Saudi Arabia. There had been riots, and many deaths. This was a region inhabited by a small minority of widely reviled non-Wahabi Muslims—they were Shi'ites, like most Iranians. Perhaps influenced by Khomeini's revolution in Iran, the Shi'ites had taken to the streets in unusual numbers that year for their annual procession to commemorate the death of the Prophet Mohamed's grandson Hussein. The religious police had intervened in the procession, we heard. The number of deaths was unknown, but an open rebellion had lasted several days. Yeslam's panic grew more hysterical, and though I tried to calm him I, too, was frightened. What would become of us all?

Then, barely three weeks after the Mecca revolt, the Soviet Union invaded Afghanistan. World events seemed to be closing in on us. Already unhinged by a neighboring revolution and a spectacular internal revolt, and enmeshed in growing radicalism in their own country, the Saudis now watched Soviet tanks rumbling through another nearby nation.

The aggressive, atheist Communist monolith had attacked a country of poor and deserving Muslims. The al-Saud princes were stunned, like everyone in the Muslim world. After weeks of inaction, the princes decided they must demonstrate that they did indeed care about fellow Muslims. They would fund the Afghan resistance.

Yeslam told me that announcements were being made in mosques to encourage ordinary people to give cash, equipment, and used clothes to the Afghans who were fighting the Soviet soldiers, and to the refugees who had begun to flee. The government announced it would give huge financial support to volunteers who went to Afghanistan to support the brave mujahideen, their brother Muslims.

Among the volunteers was my brother-in-law Osama.

Osama had just graduated from his studies when he took up the cause of the Afghans. He left quickly—there were no farewell parties. With his great stature and his inflexible opinions, Osama was an arresting figure, but he didn't seem like the best choice for a leadership position in the Afghan resistance. Nonetheless, he started to make frequent long trips to Pakistan, helping with the logistics of funneling Saudi aid to the volunteers. He helped set up clinics and training bases in Pakistan. Soon Osama more or less lived there year-round, becoming increasingly involved in the Afghan struggle.

Then Osama started moving into Afghanistan itself. According to his sisters, who spoke of him with awe, Osama was becoming a key figure in the struggle against the Soviet monolith. He imported heavy machinery, and manned earth-moving equipment to blast out tunnels through Afghanistan to house field hospitals for the fighters, and stocks of weaponry. He built dugouts to shield advancing Afghan warriors as they attacked Soviet bases. We heard that Osama had even taken up arms in man-to-man combat.

Osama was making a name for himself. He was not just the sixteenth or seventeenth Bin Laden brother any longer. He was admired. He was involved in a noble cause. Osama was a warrior—a Saudi hero.

Along with almost everyone else in Saudi Arabia, Yeslam and I gave to the Afghan struggle against the Soviet tanks. We packed up all the clothes we didn't need, and sent money.

Osama was not the only family member whose attachment to Islam was becoming more demonstrative. Some of the sisters-in-law whom I had always considered tedious and submissive surprised me now with their activism when it came to defending Islamic values. Sheikha, one of Yeslam's older sisters, even went to Afghanistan herself to distribute an enormous consignment of aid to the needy. She went with a retinue, of course, and saw no fighting. But I had to hand it to Sheikha: She wasn't just murmuring the Koran and defining correct behavior—she was brave enough to take action.

In Afghanistan, as in all wars, women were shouldering the worst of the burden. Afghanistan was like a nightmare come true for a mother: all those young women and children fleeing into camps, sitting destitute in the rain, herded like animals by rough-voiced men. It was terrible. Even worse was to come, when years later the Taliban fundamentalists took over.

Nineteen seventy-nine was a turning point for the whole Islamic world. For me it was as if a harsh spotlight had been turned on my own life. More sharply than ever, I realized that I was living in a fragile bubble, surrounded by a foreign culture that was subject to sudden outbursts and explosive violence.

I was still so young—in my mid-twenties—and we'd been married for just five years. Yet I had so many responsibilities and worries. I had to shelter my children. My mother's health had deterioriated; news of the situation in Iran seemed to have destabilized her emotionally. She refused my invitations to visit Jeddah, and I felt unable to leave Saudi Arabia.

Yeslam, meanwhile, remained agitated and fearful. He began having nightmares, waking me up at night to play backgammon to calm his nerves. I sought to reassure him. As the world beyond our walls seemed sometimes to be crashing around us, I watched my husband turning into a fretful, childish stranger.

CHAPTER 13

Yeslam

SOMETHING WAS REALLY WRONG WITH YESLAM, I realized. It was not just some passing mood. He was nervous all the time. He had nightmares. He was frightened of everything—frightened of dying, especially. He had various physical complaints that required endless tests and doctors but which never seemed to amount to anything precise: bellyaches, trouble breathing, sudden sweats of panic.

Yeslam hadn't really been happy since the Mecca revolt, I thought to myself. At first I'd thought his unhappiness was caused by the political situation in Saudi Arabia. First there was the shock of 1979, and then the unpredictable backlash, as Saudi Arabia began to swing sharply away from the path I'd thought the country would choose.

Money had changed Saudi Arabia enormously. But those sudden changes only touched the surface. Money bought many things, but they were only things; they brought with them no shift inside people's minds. The new buildings, the bigger houses, the huge modern shops and

European vacations—these things didn't seem to be leading to freedom.

Money was tugging Saudi Arabia toward the modern world, but the dour, puritanical, self-assured culture was tugging the country back to its extreme, traditional restrictions.

Wahabi Muslims believe truth lies in the literal reading of the Koran. Nobody may presume to adapt it to the modern day. Their code is strict. It regulates everything. Wahabis live their lives looking backward, as in a rearview mirror, to the time of Mohamed. After a few years of soaking in their newfound wealth, it seemed at base that Saudis did not want to change.

Perhaps there was a similar struggle going on inside Yeslam, too. He was under increasing stress. When Bakr and Salem had begun manipulating the Bin Laden Organization against Yeslam, I encouraged him to stand up for himself. A meeker woman—a Saudi woman—would have told him, "Ma'alesh, that's life," and encouraged him to stay in the position God had allotted to him, the tenth son. Yeslam could have submitted to the rule of his less competent older brothers, and taken refuge in his religion and tradition. But I was not that kind of woman—I couldn't allow it to happen. I didn't want to see him give in and submit.

I'm a fighter, and I encouraged Yeslam to fight. I urged him to confront his brothers, and to change things. I told him that he was the brightest and the best of them. It frightened me to think of Yeslam submitting to his society, to the lowly rank of tenth son in a family where nothing ever changed. I needed him to help Saudi Arabia to evolve—for my sake, and for the girls'. I couldn't change anything myself, because in Saudi Arabia there was no way I, as a woman and a foreigner, could achieve anything.

Only Yeslam, with his intelligence and his power, could give me hope that the country might yet make those crucial shifts that would bring us more freedom. Perhaps a Saudi wife would have given Yeslam more peace of mind. But I couldn't accept his weaknesses—and to be honest, I was panicking, too.

I pushed Yeslam to strike out on his own. In 1980, he simply stopped going to the office. He set up a brokerage in Jeddah and a big financial company in Switzerland, hiring a highly skilled staff to make investments for the newly rich Saudi merchants. It was a success—that became clear quite quickly. Yeslam's companies were going to do very well. I felt smug about that, and I told him, "You'll see. Salem and Bakr will be begging you to go back." They did—they offered Yeslam a salary to come back to the Bin Laden Group, the first time a family member would be paid over and above the annual dividend.

By this time, Yeslam was beginning to be worth a truly enormous amount of money. At the time I met him, Yeslam's share of the Bin Laden Organization was probably worth no more than $15 million. Most of it was tied up in the business, and it never seemed real to me.

Now, however, with the Bin Laden Organization flourishing and his own businesses taking off, Yeslam's personal worth rose to something closer to $300 million. He was one of the wealthiest of the brothers—as rich as Salem and Bakr. In practical terms, it didn't make much of a difference to our lives. We continued to fly commercial. I never bought vast amounts of haute couture. But I knew we were becoming extremely wealthy—I felt it was something Yeslam could be proud of.

But Yeslam was not happy, despite his obvious and soaring success in business. He was working more, spending long mornings at the Bin Laden headquarters, and then going to his own office after the evening prayer, working sometimes until nine or ten at night. Among the brothers, the rivalry and petty squabbling continued, and also the nasty blows below the belt that ate away at Yeslam, undermining his ego.

On the surface, his relationship with his family remained courteous. But I knew that things were tense with his brothers. One time, Yeslam said to me, "Salah used to be over here all the time. Now, when Bakr washes his hands, Salah is there holding out the towel." The cabals were out, whispering against him.

By striking out for himself, by rising above his rank, Yeslam had committed an almost unpardonable infraction of the unwritten social code.

It was not just I who had pushed Yeslam to break out from the social conventions. He was ambitious for himself, too. He responded to my encouragement because it was the direction in which he, too, wanted to grow. Yeslam had lived in the West. He saw a culture that understood you can make something of yourself on your own. But to do that, you must think and behave as a Westerner. And Yeslam was a Saudi.

If he had been encouraged more as a child, I'm convinced Yeslam's talents could have really emerged. But his mother was a fatalist. "It is the will of God" was one of her favorite phrases.

I tried to give him the encouragement I thought he needed. But the contradictions of his culture nagged at Yeslam. A Saudi—a Bin Laden—cannot confront and split from his brothers, in business or in any other way. So although part of Yeslam longed to achieve his own, individual ambitions—as a Western man would—another part of Yeslam needed to remain submissive, to occupy the space allotted to him in his tradition-bound culture.

Yeslam was split between two utterly irreconcilable impulses: the modern, Western ambitions encouraged by his life abroad, and the tradition-bound immobility of the Saudi way of life. I see that now. But then, I only saw his ailments, and a new weakness and distance in my husband.

Yeslam constantly consulted all sorts of medical specialists abroad—Saudi doctors made him nervous. I thought a psychiatrist might help him sort out the problems that I felt were more psychological than physical; but Yeslam refused to see a psychiatrist as I urged him to do.

I tried to soothe his fears, to calm his anxiety. I played countless games of nocturnal backgammon when Yeslam couldn't sleep. Then I managed to find a Western doctor in Jeddah with whom he felt at ease. Matthias Kalina was in charge of the military hospital. He and his wife, Sabine, became great friends of ours; indeed, even years later, when they had moved to Canada, Yeslam used to fly Dr. Kalina to Switzerland to discuss his health. Dr. Kalina prescribed Yeslam Temesta to calm his nervous tension. But Yeslam used to cut each pill into tiny pieces and swallow just one of the fragments—and of course that had no effect.

He became frightened of flying, so I accompanied him

everywhere, scheduling trips for the girls' school vacations so they could come along, too. (I never left them alone in Saudi Arabia, not even for a weekend.) He couldn't stand crowds. One summer we went to Los Angeles and stayed in Ibrahim's house there: In six weeks, except for the usual visits to doctors, we must have left the house only three times.

Yeslam was becoming a stranger to me. I cared for him so deeply, and relied on him so much, that I tried not to look too directly at the reality of his condition. I needed him to remain the clever, emancipated man whom I had married. I longed for the warm, attentive father, and the thoughtful, caring husband whom I once knew. I simply could not deal with the reality of this petulant, frightened stranger. I had to persuade myself these were simply moods—something temporary.

I don't think anyone apart from me could see that something was going wrong. My husband was adept at maintaining a perfectly unruffled exterior. But in reality, Yeslam was having a kind of nervous breakdown.

This led to a very personal milestone of my own. It was the summer of 1981 when I realized that I was pregnant again. We were having a family vacation in Geneva, and at first I felt so happy. It may not have been rational given my track record, but I was convinced: At last, we would have a son!

But when I rushed to Yeslam with my glad news, expecting him to be as happy as I was, he had a strange look on his face that I had never seen before. He said he had always wanted just two children. He told me that he was only just beginning to recover from his illnesses, and he couldn't cope with another child. He asked me to have an abortion.

I felt numb. My joy gave way to turmoil. I couldn't understand Yeslam. Why would he not want another child—perhaps a boy? But I wanted to help him. I believed you shouldn't force a man to become a father if that's not what he wants. Yeslam's reaction was so strong—he seemed so adamant—that I worried he would always resent the child if I went ahead with my pregnancy. Perhaps especially if the child should be another girl.

As much as I wanted this child, I agreed to have an abortion.

We returned to Saudi Arabia. I thought I could put it behind me. But I had dug a moral hole for myself that I would never be able to climb out of entirely. Although I could shut off my waking brain, I couldn't close down my dreams. I began having nightmares. Always, Wafah and Najia were taken from me. I had destroyed a child, and now I no longer deserved to be a mother.

Life was dark then. I felt I had done something terrible.

I was angry with myself: I didn't have the strength of mind to stand up to my husband. I had done everything for Yeslam, but now I felt that he had asked me for something unbearable—something he should never have asked me to do. He had behaved with unbelievable selfishness. And then, when it was clear that I was suffering, horribly, from this awful decision that he had demanded I make, Yeslam acted as though nothing important had happened. As if I had had a tooth extracted.

But I knew that what I had done was immeasurably more

awful. I had abandoned my unborn child, and my husband had abandoned us all.

We went through a bad patch after that. I felt very low. In hindsight, I realize I was depressed. Although I tried to knit a normal life together for the children, there wasn't much joy in it. I felt alone in an aching, new way. Deep down I had always thought that I could count on Yeslam. But now, though I had always been there when he needed me, he did not, or could not, give me the same support.

I couldn't understand Yeslam; and I felt he failed to try to understand me. Perhaps this was the beginning of the end.

CHAPTER 14

Little Girls

EVEN IN MY DARKEST DAYS, I TRIED AS BEST I COULD to bring up my daughters to be free—to grow up as themselves. Behind the high walls around our house, I thought I could build a small space where we could try to live normal lives—where I could attempt to reconcile the differences between my values and those of the world outside. I bought the children bicycles and roller skates, and taught them to swim in Haïfa's pool. Both girls loved music; they were constantly rehearsing and putting on little shows for Yeslam and me. All through their childhood, my funny little girls were always play-acting, dressing up and miming songs by my idol, Elvis.

But dancing lessons were an impossibility in Saudi Arabia. Music lessons were, too, although my girls were fascinated by classical music. One afternoon when she was just three, Wafah listened spellbound to an entire Tchaikovsky piano concerto that she'd asked me to put on ("Put on the 'Big music,' Mom, *la grande musique.*").

A friend of mine was visiting that afternoon; I remember

how struck she was to catch sight of Wafah, motionless and intent, almost wrapped around the speaker. She had real potential, I think—something special. But the simple, normal development of my daughters' artistic talents was out of my reach in Saudi Arabia.

I tried my best to give them the kind of childhood I had longed for. I invited foreign families with boys of their age to visit us. Sometimes they even spent the night. I wanted Wafah and little Najia to see boys as just people, like they were—the way their little cousins never could. For the Bin Laden girl cousins, boys were a foreign country, hostile and powerful—even if they had brothers. I hated to see that.

I was demanding with them as well. I knew they were materially privileged so I was determined that, from an early age, they should understand the value of work in order to appreciate the work of others. This was very important to me.

Yeslam and I seized every opportunity we could to go to Switzerland, where we'd bought a manor in a small village outside Geneva. There I lived as I wished, wore what I wanted to. I could drive myself to a movie—I could walk the streets alone. I taught the children to ski, and bought books like a madwoman, sighing as I thought of the long, dreary months in Jeddah.

I always dreaded returning to Saudi Arabia. For the children, too, the transition between our two worlds was sometimes brutal. When they were small, they would always try to tug the abaya off my face when I cloaked myself as we circled above Jeddah. Then, as they grew up, they stopped trying. I didn't know which was worse. I realized with a start one spring afternoon in 1981 that now the time was swiftly approaching when my little girls would have to go to school.

To this day, there is no legal obligation to educate girls in Saudi Arabia. Many Saudi men do not send their daughters to school, and very few of them feel it is important. Even education for boys is a relatively new development: Until World War II, there were only traditional schools, teaching Arabic, a little Islamic history, and the Koran. But in the early 1960s, Princess Iffat, the wife of King Faisal, faced down tremendous opposition from Islamic leaders and set up Saudi Arabia's first girls school, Dar el Hanan. This was where Yeslam proposed we send Wafah, aged six, and little four-year-old Najia.

I knew it would be hard for them, but I had no choice. Saudi children were not allowed to go to the foreigners' schools. Moreover, my girls were Bin Ladens. I could not isolate them from their father's culture. They had to face this challenge, and for the first time, they would be alone.

I had shielded the children from much of Saudi Arabia, and as a result they didn't even speak proper Arabic. I tried to prepare them—told them they would make friends, and learn Arabic, and that it would be lovely. I watched them enter their classes in their dark green pinafores and frilly white blouses, my heart sinking. They didn't cry.

Saudi children are bright and funny, like children everywhere. They may be spoiled by their maids and mothers; they may lack discipline; there may be nasty interactions between young boys—who know they are considered superior—and their sisters. But children are children, and it is impossible to suppress the spark of their natural intelligence.

In other ways, however, the Saudi children were different from my own. Starting when they are very young, they are trained to adhere to a strict social code. The certainty of women's inferior status and subservience is bred into their bones as they grow. In the car, Haïfa's older son—who was only ten or twelve—would instruct her sharply to veil if he saw men coming. Little girls knew they must walk, dress, and talk unobtrusively. They had to be submissive, docile, and obedient: It was common to see a young boy walk into a room and motion his older sister off her chair.

At school, what those children met was a form of brainwashing. I watched it happen to my daughters. Lessons—Arabic, math, history—were learned by rote, parrot-fashion, with no deeper understanding of their real content. There were no sports, no debates, no discussions. No games, marbles, or tricycles. Religious education was the most important class of all, and it seemed to take up half or more of every day.

When Wafah was seven or eight, I remember, I looked through her exercise book one evening and I found she'd written down, "I hate Jews. I love Palestine," in her childish Arabic script. What was happening to my daughter? If she was going to hate somebody, I wanted her to have a good reason. The Arab-Israeli dispute was something she knew nothing about.

The next day I went to the school principal and said, "My daughter doesn't know where Palestine is. She knows nothing about Israel. She isn't even doing geography yet.

How can she be taught to hate when she doesn't know anything about it?"

The principal, a small but imperious woman, was completely impervious to my protest. "This is not a matter for you to discuss," she told me. "You are a foreigner, you cannot understand. Does your husband know about this?"

I tried to remain dignified. I said my husband was completely aware of my position, and that I would ask him to phone her. Then I went home, called Yeslam, and had him phone the school and tell the principal that I was in full charge of the children's education.

It was a kind of victory—I wanted her to know that Yeslam gave me full authority over the children, something few other Saudi wives could claim. But I knew deep down that I could do nothing to prevent the school from trying to teach my girls to blindly hate along with reading and writing. I had no choice. I must merely hand them over from 8:00 a.m. to 2:00 p.m. every day. I just had to accept this, and it became one of a long list of things I began accepting against my will.

Still, although I could not change their schoolwork, I was their mother—I could influence my children. I began a conscious effort to teach the girls how to reason—how to deduce things, how to think for themselves. I would pick them up from school at two, and over lunch we would often discuss the news, or religious tolerance—at a child's level, naturally. I laid out a program for after-school activities— structured play, with Playmobil and plasticine, and sports. The girls would learn music. Perhaps, I mused, I should hire a tutor to come to the house.

I didn't care that Wafah got high marks in school: I knew that her teacher would always give a Bin Laden the best marks, whether she deserved it or not. Everything was glossed over in that way. And in any case, her grades only reflected Wafah's quick memory—not her understanding of her lessons.

One day, exasperated, I met with her classroom teacher and told her I wanted her to treat Wafah the same as the others. A few days later, Wafah came home sobbing: Her teacher had hit her across the face. I went back to the teacher, not to make a big protest, but to say simply that I thought this was not the best method of discipline. Irate, the woman said Wafah was a liar—she had never done such a thing. She asked the children—"Wafah is lying, isn't she? I didn't hit her, did I?" But one brave child, another half-foreigner, raised her hand, and said Wafah had told the truth. That poor little girl had a miserable time for the rest of the school year.

I quickly understood that my intervention in school was doing no good, but I couldn't watch my children become educated in this way. Though I hated to load the girls down with extra work, I hired a female teacher to tutor them after school, and told her I wanted my children to understand, not memorize, their lessons. The teacher never asked me what I meant—a Saudi does not say she doesn't understand, because it would mean losing face. But I could see she was struggling to figure it out. And I think in the end she realized it was a better way to learn. It certainly saved my little Wafah's and Najia's brains.

On another occasion, Wafah came home crying again.

There had been music in school, and she had begun dancing. A schoolmate hissed at her to stop. "It's *haram*," she told Wafah. "Dancing is *haram*. Don't you know anything?" What do you do when your child asks you if dancing is a sin? "Dancing is not *haram*," I soothed her. "You can dance."

I could have warned her to dance at home, in private. These things might get her into trouble one day. But how can you tell your children that music and dancing are sinful? These countless, endless, foolish, mean little restrictions chafed at me. I couldn't force them on my daughters.

I treasured my children; I tried to give them my love, acknowledging that they had their own thoughts. Around me, though, I saw a completely different kind of upbringing. In Saudi Arabia, there is a different vision of respect. You never see a child contradict his father. For me, respect goes deeper than that—Mary Martha's example had taught me this. I think that the more you love someone, the more you should be able to say difficult things—superficial agreement is for strangers. I wanted my children to know more than me, to be cleverer than me, to disagree with me and show it.

I respected my children's characters and opinions, just as much as I wanted them to respect mine. Respect to me had become something that I should try to earn by my actions. I didn't want my children to feel they were obliged to accept all my ideas. I didn't want them to be cowed. I wanted them to say no to me, because if they could do that they could say no to the world—and grow up to become the people they wanted to be.

But at school, my girls learned the fear of hellfire. They began to worry about my soul. "If you don't pray, Mommy, you'll go to hell," Najia would say, staring up at me with her big, innocent eyes. It hurt me horribly, every time, to see the worry in her eyes. I would say my faith was a matter between God and me. That the most important thing was to behave in a way that helped others, and not harmed them. I told my little girls I didn't want them to pray because they were frightened of hell. Prayer is not something you do for bargaining with God, I would explain: It is an intimate search for inner peace.

It was a topic that I broached from time to time with some of my sisters-in-law. Ultimately it was pointless, however—their certitude was absolute. But with my children, the lesson sank in—perhaps too well. Despite their young age they were able to form their own opinions. One day the King decreed that all the nannies in Saudi Arabia would have to become Muslim. Our Filipina maid, Dita, told Wafah and Najia. She said she was ashamed that the King said her religion was not correct. Wafah asked her if she believed in Islam, and then drew herself up in shock when Dita said she didn't. "Why would you change if you still believe in your religion?" she asked Dita. "What will your mummy and daddy think of you? My mummy will never make you change your religion, you know."

I thought it was darling, and also rather deep and clear-sighted of my little daughter, and that Friday when we lunched with my mother-in-law I told her the story. Om Yeslam's reaction was unexpected. Frowning, she told me, "You have closed her door to paradise." Wafah, at seven, had realized that Dita's belief was the issue—not the appearance of believing. But my mother-in-law was convinced that pretending to be a Muslim was infinitely preferable to being a believing Catholic.

I began to fear that by bringing the children up with Western ideas I was doing them no favors. Slowly, imperceptibly, it seemed we were developing two different mind-sets, along with our two different wardrobes for Switzerland and for Saudi Arabia. In Geneva the children wore little T-shirts and frilly short-shorts, and I wore a bikini at the seaside in Cannes. They went horseback-riding and learned to water-ski. Yeslam permitted it all because they were young—it didn't matter. And they were abroad, so it somehow didn't count.

But clothes that looked fine in Geneva simply could not be worn in Jeddah—not even inside my home. With the people who mattered, appearances had to be maintained. I had to be careful. I watched as the children's older cousins wore skirts that were longer and more demure. As they grew older, fewer girl cousins attended Wafah's and Najia's birthday parties. It was no longer proper that they play boisterously with boys. Many of those who did come were stiff— not like children anymore. They no longer knew how to scream and run around, or play, or dance.

My children were beginning to enter a world that was not mine. The first time I saw one of their cousins wearing a veil I yelped, "Already?" The abstract idea that my children were growing up was becoming more real. Soon it would be Wafah's turn to cloak herself in darkness. There was a little leeway: Very religious families would veil their girls at nine, but others waited until puberty, at twelve or thirteen. But every girl had to veil in public once she had her first period. I dreaded the day, though I tried to reason with myself. After all, *I* wore the abaya myself: It was not the end of the world, merely a foolish inconvenience.

But watching as Saudi society seemed to drift deeper into rigid fanaticism, I could no longer be confident that one day my daughters would be permitted to choose *not* to wear the veil if they wished. I looked at my own abaya, trimmed with faint silver embroidery: It seemed, suddenly, a hideous garment, ghastly in its blackness and terrifying in all it represented. I realized that by bringing my children up to believe in freedom, tolerance, and equality, I was shaping them into women who would rebel from a society seeking to lock them in. And as Princess Mish'al's murder had amply demonstrated, in Saudi Arabia a rebellious woman may be marked for death.

I was a foreigner, and my husband was gentle and understanding. But no other Bin Laden—none of the Saudi men I knew—could have tolerated my Western values. Would Wafah and Najia have as easy a life as I did? Or would their husbands be more like the dour, reserved Bakr? Like Mahrouz, the former playboy turned Islamic hard-line extremist? Or, an appalling thought, like rigidly puritanical Osama? Saudi men were so unpredictable: An apparent liberal could shift position in a few months, become devout, and impose strict Islamic mores on his wife.

I had chosen my husband. I received men in my home, and had dinner parties. Would my children be able to make the same choices? Or would they marry a cousin, perhaps, in a family arrangement, and be delivered to him, mind and body, come what may, for the rest of their lives?

My daughters' marriages could break down; my own marriage might fail one day. That idea takes on even bigger significance in Saudi Arabia, where your husband holds the key to the only tiny freedoms a woman can hope for.

The word "Islam" means submission. I had come to dread submission. I had seen too many women deprived of their children, their independence, their own minds. But if my girls were not submissive, what lives would they have?

It gnawed at me. I had been free to choose, and I had chosen a life that was restricted in many small ways, along with some big ones. By making that choice, however, I had ensured that my daughters would not be free to choose as I had chosen. In my nightmares I saw my little girls growing up to become Saudi women—bent over under the weight of their subservience, cloaked in darkness. In those long evenings, as I faced the dusk outside my terrace, I no longer even saw the black birds flying across the empty desert. Now it was my worries that wheeled around my head, nagging at me.

CHAPTER 15

A Saudi Couple

As Yeslam's behavior grew stranger, I also came to feel increasingly distant from the Bin Laden family. I lived for the school vacations—counting the days till we could head for Europe, or the United States, and my own version of freedom. Still, when Fawzia, Yeslam's younger sister, became engaged to be married, it was inevitable that her giving-away ceremony would be conducted at our Jeddah house. Just as Yeslam was my legal guardian, he was her head of family, too.

Of all the women in the Bin Laden family, I was most familiar with Fawzia. I had watched her grow up and become a woman. She was Yeslam's only full sister, Om Yeslam's only daughter, and we lived in the same house for over a year. Because she was a girl, Fawzia had never been sent abroad to boarding school; she had always lived with her mother, and until she was married the two of them even shared a bedroom.

Fawzia had a mighty view of her own importance. She was pretty—she considered herself the prettiest of the Bin

Laden sisters. As a full sister, she always felt that she should have greater importance in her brothers' lives than their wives did.

I should have been close to Fawzia, but I couldn't be—I felt that she envied my special relationship with her brother. She realized I wasn't blind to the wiles she used to obtain concessions from her future husband or even her brothers.

For me, relationships are straightforward. If I wanted something from Yeslam, I would ask him directly. When my mother encountered financial difficulties, I simply asked Yeslam to help her, which he did. I was outspoken about the things I felt really mattered, and Yeslam and I could openly debate them.

Fawzia had been brought up to avoid that kind of clear, direct behavior. Like many other Saudi women, she had learned how to manipulate men in a subtler, more oblique manner to obtain what she needed. If they wanted to go overseas, they would always come up with a plausible excuse, like a medical appointment. If they needed more money, to buy something, they'd invent some household bill as a pretext, then use the money for their own devices.

My sisters-in-law, out of fear of being left in a difficult financial situation one day, routinely squirreled money away from their household budgets, to use as a private war chest. One time, I had presents to buy for friends overseas, and Yeslam gave me 200,000 riyals (about $50,000) to go to the gold souk. I went shopping with one of my sisters-in-law, and when we got back I showed Yeslam what we'd chosen, adding, "There's 60,000 riyals left over." I put the money on the side table. My sister-in-law was surprised. She chided me, "Your husband gave you that money. You should keep it for yourself!"

But Yeslam and I never lived that way. There was almost always a box of cash in the house—200,000 riyals, or sometimes ten times that much—that I could use as I wanted. Why should I do something so underhanded?

I never remember seeing a Saudi woman being direct, or admitting ignorance. Sometimes I would be talking with my sisters-in-law and realize they had absolutely no knowledge of what I was talking about, but they would never own up to it. (Later I might overhear them repeating it to someone else, though.) Saudi women never openly admire something that belongs to someone else either. They denigrate people, their looks, their way of dressing, their household. But then they copy them constantly—even as they express their scorn.

Fawzia and I came from two different worlds. Perhaps her background and her place in that male-dominated society meant that she simply had to learn to be manipulative and sly, in order to get what she needed. I had learned, in America, to be straightforward. In Saudi Arabia, her behavior was probably more intelligent and better adapted than mine.

There were so many differences between us. I'm a woman, and I admit I can be vain. I, too, like luxury—the things that money can buy. In those days I had five or six fur coats for my trips to Europe, a safeful of jewelry, and a walk-in wardrobe filled with prêt à porter dresses. I never asked the price of anything—if something attracted me, I bought it.

But for so many Saudi women, shopping was like a compulsion—a frenzy to fill the emptiness and boredom of their lives. They didn't seem to buy things because they appealed to them. They bought them because other women had them, and they wanted more, and better, stuff than everyone else. Once, Yeslam gave me an emerald necklace. Fawzia sniffed at it; then she went straight out and bought one, too.

Still, when Fawzia was getting married, I was happy for her: She and Om Yeslam seemed so thrilled. We were in Geneva when we heard that arrangements had been finalized for her engagement to Majid al-Suleiman, from one of the important Saudi families. She told me she needed a dress, and I rushed out and bought her a beautiful one from Givenchy. It was pink and white, with silk ribbons, the bridal dress from the latest haute couture collection, the most beautiful dress in Geneva that year.

Fawzia turned her nose up at the dress—it was too simple—but when she saw that the sisters-in-law loved it, she wore it anyway. I don't remember her thanking me, though. She was so sure of her own superiority. It always came down to the same thing—she was a Saudi, and I wasn't.

For Fawzia's *melka*, the engagement party, we pulled out all the stops. We strung the garden with thousands of lights, and laid out plans to serve hundreds of women. But then, the night before the wedding, Fawzia threatened to call it off. She wanted a marriage contract that would ensure she could initiate a divorce.

I had never heard of such a thing. In Saudi Arabia, divorce is simple—if you're a man. He merely recites "I divorce you," three times, in the presence of witnesses, and the thing is done. A woman, however, must struggle through the byzantine procedures at a religious court, and her only hope for divorce is on the grounds of manifestly un-Islamic behavior. (Adultery and beatings don't count.)

The *melka* was postponed for two days. The florists took back the enormous flower displays; everything went on hold. But Fawzia got her contract and the party went ahead. As the guests arrived and threw off their abayas, it was like a competition for who could wear the heaviest makeup, the most jewelry, the most expensive haute couture dress. Fawzia and the groom, Majid, arrived separately, to the ululating calls of the women present. They were seated under a canopy. They signed the register. This was the part of my own wedding that I had missed—I had signed the register in the car—because Regaih's *melka* had happened before I arrived in Saudi Arabia to be married. Fawzia's actual wedding party took place weeks later, in a hotel. For now, though, Fawzia and Majid were legally engaged and finally had the right to spend time together without a chaperone.

Yeslam and I liked Majid. He was twenty-two, a bit younger than his wife, handsome, with classic features and a beautiful smile. He was a very sweet-tempered man, much more tolerant of others than Fawzia was. Majid was witty—he had a great sense of humor. We talked and laughed together; in the summer, when we went to Geneva, we went about in a foursome. Once, he saw me wearing a silver fox coat, with a natural gray sheen. Majid, who loved being playful, exclaimed, "What, you gave the poor animal gray hair?"

He looked over at Yeslam, and said, "Careful, man, don't stay too close to your wife, you'll be getting gray hair, too!"

Wafah and Najia adored Majid. He was such a kind and patient man, and it was a good thing Fawzia had Majid, to keep her in check. One time, I remember, Fawzia, Majid, and I were getting ready to leave their house to go somewhere. Majid and I were waiting downstairs, and he visibly winced as he heard Fawzia reprimanding the maid, who had burned a hole in the carpet while ironing on the floor. "Why not just buy the poor woman an ironing board?" I thought to myself.

Fawzia had two little children, Sarah, and later, baby Faisal. Like so many wealthy Saudi children, little Sarah was indulged in material ways but she never really got much sustained adult attention. She had boxes of toys she didn't know how to play with, and almost no discipline. I remember one time watching as little Sarah tore up packs and packs of playing cards: Fawzia never tried to teach her respect for objects or people.

Saudi parents seem so besotted with their children, but at the same time they overlook their deeper needs. Sarah never seemed occupied by anything constructive. If she got fussy, Fawzia would just wave her over to the maid—not a trained nanny or anything, just a household servant. This woman looked after Sarah—and Faisal, the baby—from morning to night, in addition to doing the household chores. If a child cried, it was the maid's fault, and there was never a word of gratitude for her work. Dita, our Filipina maid, used to help my children fall asleep by lying down next to them on the bed. This simple domestic ritual became a problem if the girls ever napped at Fawzia's house, as Fawzia's maid was not permitted to use the furniture. She wasn't even allowed to sit on a chair while feeding the children.

Majid was a moderating influence on his wife. But one day, tragedy struck. Majid had a passion for automobiles and he bought himself a Formula One racing car. It was bright green, and known to all: It raced under the colors of the Saudi airline, and was the pride and joy of every teenage boy in the country. The day the car was delivered, Majid decided to drive it. But the car's acceleration was far too powerful, and driving out of the garage it jerked forward. Majid's head was thrown backward, against the roll bar, and he was knocked unconscious.

They took Majid to the university hospital, where he revived. A doctor sewed up the bleeding wound at the back of his head. But he was hemorrhaging internally, and he soon lost consciousness again. Neurosurgeons were flown in from London, but it was too late: Majid's brain stopped functioning. His body followed a month later. He was wrapped in a simple shroud and buried at sunset, in an unmarked grave, in the desert, as the Wahabis do. No women were permitted to be present.

I was completely devastated, and I could think of nothing else. Majid, so sweet-natured and funny, was only twenty-seven. How could he be dead? I prepared for the three-day mourning period at Majid's mother's, when all the women in her family would be present, to accompany Om Majid and Fawzia in their grief. (Yeslam went, with the men, to Majid's father's side.) When I got there I found a roomful of women wailing loudly, dressed all in black or in white, and Fawzia in full makeup on the sofa. She had recently given birth—Faisal, her son, was just two or three months old—and when Om Yeslam asked if she needed anything, Fawzia said, "A girdle."

I was dumbstruck. To be worried about your appearance at a time like that! I expressed my sympathy for her loss. "It's God's will," Fawzia told me. "Maybe it's all for the best. Perhaps if he had lived he would have divorced me and taken my children."

Again appalled, I tried to focus on the children. Faisal, the baby, was crying: He hadn't been bathed or even attended to much for days. I took him and washed him, and then I took little Sarah out to a merry-go-round, to distract her. I spent the three-day mourning period as silently as possible.

One of Majid's sisters was distraught, and I told Fawzia I was worried about her. "Oh her," Fawzia said. "During our five years of marriage, we hardly ever saw her. She's being melodramatic." It was as if Fawzia didn't want anyone else to feel what she manifestly wasn't feeling.

A few days later, we got the news that one of Om Yeslam's brothers had died in Iran. Fawzia was all over Om Yeslam— "Oh Mama, poor Mama"—and I'm afraid I couldn't stop myself. "Fawzia, how long has it been since Om Yeslam has seen her brother?" I asked her. She threw me a look that would melt ice, sharp as a snake, and I think after that she really did hate me.

A few days later, before leaving for Geneva, I decided to express my regrets one last time to Om Majid—she was a gentle woman, and I liked her. Fawzia asked my driver to carry over a note. When the note was handed over to Om Majid, I saw her wave to her houseboy. "Give the driver the money," she said, her face still worn by grief. It took me a few moments to realize that Fawzia had sent over to her mother-in-law the 2,000 riyal bill for Fawzia's cook's salary. I wanted to sink into the floor.

CHAPTER 16

Sisters in Islam

FAWZIA NEVER SHOWED ANY EVIDENCE OF COMPAS-
sion in her soul, but she prayed five times a day. All the
Bin Laden women did; and among the most orthodox of all
was Sheikha. Sheikha was close in both blood and spirit to
Osama, though far more meek, of course. The younger Bin
Laden women all admired her. Even the mothers-in-law
looked up to Sheikha for her religious devotion, particularly after she began working for Osama, collecting aid for
the Afghans—and traveling to Afghanistan to deliver it.

I visited Sheikha often, as I did many of my sisters-in-law.
I needed to understand the culture my children lived in,
and my husband's roots. Sheikha and her husband had
built a house near ours. But we were never intimate in the
Western sense. Saudi women don't open their lives to each
other as American or European women do—and especially
not to a foreigner.

Among the women, I found there was a more codified
sense of full sisters and half-sisters than there was among
the men. Ahmad's three sisters, for example—who shared

the same mother—did seem to be close: They went about everywhere together. Sometimes the Bin Laden sisters seemed truly friendly even if they were only half-sisters: Sheikha and Rafah, for example, did not have the same mother, but they shared each other's religious convictions. But I had not grown up with them; I was not even a half-sister—I was just a sister-in-law, and a Westerner at that. So I can't say I was ever what you would call close.

Still, I would visit. It was an activity. Sheikha would ask me for news of Yeslam; I would politely inquire about the health of her family. Even this simple dialogue was ritualized, a minefield of hideous possible errors. Sheikha could use my husband's name in conversation: She was his sister. But I could not speak the name of Sheikha's husband, even though she was my sister-in-law. To use his name out loud, or ask about his health: That would presume a form of intimacy. That was something you could never do.

I had lived so long in Saudi Arabia that I no longer noticed these stiff, polite rituals of segregation. Looking back on it now, I see how strange and alienating they really were.

Despite everything, I was fond of Sheikha—she had energy and vigor, though it all went into pursuing her religious beliefs. Sheikh Mohamed's oldest daughter, Aïsha, also had a quite energetic and commanding appeal. Aïsha was very close to Om Yeslam—they had breast-fed each other's children—and all the Bin Laden women seemed to accord Aïsha a special place, as befit the oldest of the great Sheikh's daughters. (Aïsha was older than many of his wives.)

Aïsha was short, but very dignified, and also relatively outspoken. When I arrived at her house, Aïsha would often complain that Yeslam didn't come by to see her more often. It was daring—no other sister would ever complain about a brother.

But the implied criticism never went too far. One time I arrived at some family gathering with Yeslam, and spotted Aïsha in the room. "Look, you don't have to tell me about Yeslam not coming to see you anymore," I said to her. "He's here! You can tell him yourself!" The whole group was aghast. I had invited Aïsha to take my husband—her brother—to task, in public! The silence that followed my remark seemed endless.

The only break in the terribly proper protocol that ruled relationships among the Bin Laden women was a small, but perceptible, jealousy of one of the sisters, Randa. Randa was unmarried and an only child—she had no full brothers; nevertheless, she was privileged because she was Salem's favorite, and Salem was the oldest brother.

Salem never refused Randa anything, or so the women said. It was almost scandalous, they muttered, the way Salem took her everywhere, traveling with her even outside the country—sometimes, even without his wife. In fact, they whispered, if Salem traveled abroad with Randa and took his wife along, Randa would sit beside him in the car while his wife was relegated to the back seat.

I have always hated gossip, and this sort of tittle-tattle seemed particularly futile.

You might think that in a world of women, there would be companionship and spontaneity, a warm, supportive understanding. But among the Bin Laden women every gesture was always very proper, highly ritualized, and almost completely static. My friend Haïfa—Bakr's Syrian wife— had a more natural understanding of the proper codes than I did, and she had to help me learn them.

I was a good social mimic. I did eventually manage to perform the correct conversational rituals at the endless afternoon gatherings I felt obliged to attend.

But they frustrated me. Nothing ever seemed to go deeper. It was such a large family, with such an enormous amount of to-ing and fro-ing, but the contact between them seemed so superficial.

Then, one afternoon, Sheikha invited me to attend one of her religious study meetings. The chosen sisters filed into her living room and listened quietly while a woman scholar droned on, reading and interpreting the Koran. Some of these women were becoming downright fanatical, I noticed. You could tell who the fervent ones were by their gloves, thick and black in the Jeddah heat. Many wore headscarves all the time now—even inside the house, although only women were present.

The force of their religious conviction gave some of these women a leadership role—Aïsha, Sheikha, and Rafah, another, rather pretty, older sister. I think that Rafah was genuinely concerned about my immortal soul, while I wanted her to open up a little to the wider world. Rafah and I often debated the merits of Saudi Islam's restrictions. She was always preaching the correct Islamic behavior—she was the one who had so strenuously objected to celebrating my daughters' birthdays. The younger women—like Osama's dismal, retiring young wife, Najwah—would always voicelessly agree.

I did genuinely like some of those women. Om Yeslam was kind and gentle. I enjoyed Sheikha's energy. Rafah's mother, like Sheikha's, was sweet and welcoming; Taiba, who had lost her children when her husband divorced her, was gentle and warm. I think they liked me, too.

Still, attending that religious study meeting in Sheikha's house that afternoon, I realized how deeply in the minority Haïfa and I had become. I watched the women seated around me, and listened to them talk, as if they were in a movie. I felt like a complete outsider. Najwah was particularly unsettling—perhaps because she was so meek. She was constantly pregnant—by the time I left Saudi Arabia for good, she and Osama had had seven sons and she was not yet thirty. With drab clothes and downcast eyes, Najwah seemed almost completely invisible.

What could I talk about with women like this? What can you say to someone when you have nothing in common? There I was, thinking to myself, "What does this girl have in her life? She is pious . . . Religion is her entire world . . . She cannot listen to music . . . She bears children and her husband doesn't let her out." She might smile at me, probably thinking to herself, "Poor woman, she will go to hell." And I was thinking, "Poor woman, she is *living* in hell"—we had totally opposing convictions. Najwah and her kind frightened me. I consider women to be the guardians of moral progress, entrusted with the future; when they hold on to the past out of fear of change, a society cannot evolve.

It seems to me that Islam, more than any other religion, bites deeply into the everyday life of a believer. It is not just a theology; it is a vastly detailed way of life. To a strictly orthodox Muslim—and the Saudis are the strictest kind of Muslim there is—no separation of religion and state is conceivable. Islam is about Islamic law: The code of behavior and law is as fundamental to religious practice as the Koran. The Sharia—the body of Islamic law—is the constitution of Saudi Arabia. There is simply no possibility that the government, or Saudi society, could ever be divorced from the strict rules of Wahabi Islam.

Sheikh Mohamed bin Abdul Wahab, who reinvigorated Saudi Islam in the 1700s with his extreme puritan revivalism, was convinced that the Islam he saw around him needed to be purified—to be taken back to its seventh-century roots. Whereas in other, less-isolated Islamic countries, like Egypt, Islam was seen as a set of concepts more or less in evolution through the centuries, Sheikh Wahab insisted that no interpretation of the Prophet's law could be permitted. Islam was to be taken whole. It could not be modernized or reassembled.

As a result, the Saudis have become the guardians of absolute orthodoxy in the Islamic world—the hardest of the hard. The only difference between Saudi Islam and that of the ultra-hard-line Afghan Taliban is the opulence and private self-indulgence of the al-Sauds. The Saudis are the Taliban, in luxury.

Living in a modern, global economy means that the Saudis have had to change in at least some ways, and to adapt their society, no matter how slightly. But even simple innovations, like automobiles, or photographic images, or television, require rulings from Islamic scholars to determine whether or not they are permissible under Islam. Partly to pacify the people who are angered by such modern changes—and also partly out of simple conviction—the Saudis fund movements to export their strict Wahabi form of Islam to the outside world. Funding such movements became a particularly intense concern after the Soviet invasion of Afghanistan.

When I was living in Saudi Arabia, it was always said that 6 percent of oil revenue went to propagate Islam around the world. In addition to that official spending, great families feel a personal duty to sponsor evangelical Islamic movements. So mosques in Europe, in Asia, in the United States, are built and funded by Saudi Arabia. Their preachers adopt the hard-line message of Sheikh Wahab, preaching to Muslim cultures that have evolved to become more tolerant and more flexible.

Scholars are brought to Riyadh and Jeddah to be educated, and return to their homelands to spread the word. The Saudis pressure the people who receive their financial aid to enforce strict rules—to ban alcohol, impose fasting during Ramadan, and minimize the education of women and their access to the workforce. Saudi Arabian Islam is an enormous, very wealthy power that seeks to change the world, and it stretches far outside the borders of that otherwise firmly closed country.

Saudi Arabia is the cradle of Islam—the homeland of the Prophet Mohamed—and Saudi Islam is constructed around the need to safeguard the Prophet's teaching and the holy sites of Mecca and Medina, where he lived. The presence of infidels is intolerable. As the years went by, I came to see how incredibly defensive Saudi society is about other religions.

Even the country's flag boldly announces "There Is No God But Allah." No religion other than Islam may be practiced in the country. No Bibles may be brought in; no collective prayer is permitted. Many foreign workers, such as Dita, my Christian Filipina maid, suffer great pain from this ruling.

In other ways, too, Saudi Arabia exerts an almost paranoid control over the millions of foreigners it must import to design and operate the machinery of modern life. Except for diplomats, every foreigner who enters the Kingdom must be sponsored by a Saudi, who takes his passport for "safekeeping," and who exerts enormous control over his actions. No foreigner can even leave the country without the permission of his sponsor: Getting an exit visa requires the sponsor's signature. Foreigners may not own property in the country, and in order to go into business they must have a Saudi partner.

Women who marry Saudis often find themselves trapped in the country: Their husband—or ex-husband—will not permit them, or their children, to leave. Without his signature, there can be no exit visa; without an exit visa, there is simply no route out.

Living in Saudi Arabia I always felt somehow clandestine, as though I had sneaked into the country under false pretenses and could never show my true nature. When I looked at women like Najwah, or Rafah and Sheikha, I was afraid for my daughters. These women did not chafe at the restrictions they lived under: They embraced them. Even after many years in the country, I could only hazily understand that terrible, self-enslaving mind-set.

At the time, I thought my children's destiny lay in Saudi

Arabia. I loved my husband; we lived in his country; my girls were Saudi. I knew that I should teach them the codes of behavior that would ease their lives there as adults. They must learn—and learn as young as possible—to operate as Saudi women. Their well-being and peace of mind might depend on this, as well as countless small freedoms that required male permission.

Still, try as I might, I never could manage to teach my daughters to practice the manipulative, underhanded behavior that characterized the women around me. Perhaps, for the children's good, I should have made that effort, but I felt powerless to prepare them for lives as Saudi women. I hated even thinking about it.

When I could bring myself to reflect on Wafah's and Najia's future, I realized that I was raising my children to become rebels in Saudi society. I knew they might suffer for that. But I was also afraid, deep down, that my girls would become like Najwah and the others—that they would adopt the way of strict religion, and leave me. I didn't want my children to become black-gloved, mute strangers: That I could not have borne. I would not have wanted my sweet, gay little girls to grow up that way.

Najwah was a submissive person by nature, I think, and her upbringing had made her fatalistic. She never permitted herself to want more from her life than obedience to her husband and father. It would drive me crazy: I would think, "God gave you arms and legs and a head to think with, so use them." I found myself becoming frustrated, as a woman, to be surrounded by women who simply did not have the courage to resist the system.

Sheikha and Rafah did have courage, only they threw it all into religion. I think that was simpler for them than fighting for their rights as human beings. Piety gave them the illusion that they had power. I think they believed that if they were very strictly religious, then the men—like the other women—would respect that. It seemed to work— religious women did get much more respect than the Westernized ones, like Hassan's Lebanese wife, Leila.

For women like Sheikha and Rafah, I'm sure their fierce piety was a matter of personal conviction. But it was also partly a necessary tactic for them, I think. When you live as a complete dependent, you have to learn how to influence your master: There may be no other way you can survive.

Another way a Saudi woman can hope to influence the men who control her is to manipulate her children, particularly the boys. Women were always more indulgent with their sons, and I noticed that when a husband was around, they would be even more attentive. If you were a fine mother, then your husband would never divorce you—that was the theory. And a son would one day be your legal guardian in your husband's place. A husband might stray, or die, or divorce you, but a devoted son would always stand by his mother.

I didn't have sons. And the other Bin Laden women— even Om Yeslam—didn't seem to care much about my daughters' upbringing. I would do the dutiful daughter-in-law thing, and prattle on. There was no other subject for neutral discussion, in those long, tedious afternoon tea parties. I would report that Wafah and Najia had learned to pray, that I had taken them to Mecca, that they had learned

Arabic and could recite this or that section of the Koran. But Om Yeslam never inquired about such issues. I couldn't help thinking that she cared far more for Fawzia's little girl, Sarah.

I was trying to make her love my children, but I don't think I ever managed to. Perhaps, at base, it was because I was a foreigner. One day, much later on, when Yeslam and I had moved into a larger house in Jeddah, Wafah was playing with a little half-English school friend, running around the house screaming and wet from the pool.

"Ah, that foreign girl," snapped Om Yeslam, exasperated.

I answered her back rather tersely: "We are all foreigners to somebody."

"Not me," Om Yeslam answered, looking straight at me. "There is not one drop of Christian blood in me."

I did have a drop of Christian blood in me—my father's. And so did the girls. And what Om Yeslam really meant was that I had the determined, willful personality that comes from living as an individual, in the West. She felt that I simply would never bring myself to submit in the proper manner— to Islam, to the rules of Saudi society, or to my husband.

And she was right.

CHAPTER 17

Princes and Princesses

I MET MY DEAR FRIEND LATIFA IN GENEVA, AT A LUNCH one day with Fawzia and Majid. Socializing in Saudi Arabia is complicated—could women sit at a table with a man they hadn't met?—but Saudis do let part of their complex web of restrictions drop when they are abroad, and men and women can see each other in Europe a little more freely. Yeslam and Latifa's husband, Turki, enjoyed each other's company. We became friendly, the four of us, and Latifa and I became close.

Latifa was an al-Saud: a princess. I had met Saudi princesses before, and I hadn't been particularly impressed— the few I'd met had been trite, and unbearably superior. But Latifa was not that kind of person. She was interested in other people. She didn't have the arrogance of some of the other Saudi royals.

Latifa was tall, and had a languid poise—she was one of the most beautiful women I had ever met. She was very different from me—very quiet. I used to joke, "Latifa, the walls are tired of hearing only my voice." She was so reserved that we never spoke much about the ruling family—which was her family—or political events.

But Latifa liked having an outsider around, someone who had no part in the shifting mass of courtiers within the royal family intrigues. And I liked her, because I saw in her a true Arabian princess. Not just because of her striking beauty, but because something inside Latifa was noble in a very deep sense.

Latifa's husband, Turki, was a member of the al-Saud royal family, too, but he was shy and rather formal. In the beginning, even after he became friendly with Yeslam, he found it hard to be alone in a room with me. The first time Turki came to our house in Saudi Arabia and found that Yeslam hadn't yet arrived home I had to practically force him to wait inside. Turki sat bolt upright on the living room sofa, not daring to look me in the face. It was one thing to see me unveiled in Geneva; it was quite another to be alone with me in a room in Jeddah.

Turki loved being in the West—he loved the relaxation of restrictions, and the freedom to be yourself and socialize naturally with women as well as men. But in Saudi Arabia he snapped back to custom. Now that I'd lived in Saudi Arabia for so long, I could see that it was hard for Turki, too, to resolve the contradictions of living in two worlds.

Prince Turki was one of the few Saudi men I truly liked. Later, when I left Saudi Arabia for good, he gave me his support. I will always be grateful to him for that. Latifa, too, has been loyal—she is the only Saudi woman who has stood by me to this day.

Latifa and Turki lived in the compound of Turki's father,

in one of several mansions he'd built for his children. They were not palaces: Both Latifa and Turki were royals, but they were not from the major branch of the al-Saud family that might one day inherit the throne—Yeslam told me he probably had more money than they did.

Latifa's father, Prince Mansur, was a respected older relative of King Khaled's. When he traveled, Prince Mansur would request the use of the King's own airplane—one of the several that contained a fully equipped operating room on board and countless servants. It was not easy to say no to Prince Mansur.

Prince Mansur was a strict man, and he was accustomed to demanding complete obedience from his daughter. When Latifa was eight years old, her father divorced her mother, who was then banished. Latifa didn't see her again until after she married Turki, who permitted his new wife to contact her mother.

Even as an adult, Latifa would obey her father's directives unquestioningly. Once, her father felt that Latifa had been in Europe for too long and demanded that she return to Jeddah right away. At the time, he was visiting one of his properties in Spain, so it wasn't that he wanted to see her. Even though her husband was in Europe with her, Latifa went back to Jeddah at her father's command. She was gentle, and clear-sighted, but obedience had been bred into every cell of her body.

Latifa was a wonderful person, but she was also a good Saudi woman. And this was the kind of respect a good Saudi owed to the family patriarch. Nobody contradicts the patriarch. Not even an adult son, with a family of his own, would dare disobey—much less a daughter.

If she'd lived in Europe, Latifa could have made use of her intelligence—she could have been strong and free. She could have developed her personality so much further. But, brought up in Saudi Arabia, her character was weakened, stifled into submission. She was very fatalistic. If something went wrong, she would say, "There's no point thinking about it, it's done." There was no revolt left in Latifa. She'd learned to stop asking questions. I think her spirit had been broken.

Latifa had known Princess Mish'al, the young girl who was killed by her grandfather for falling in love. That was one of the issues that she never wanted to think about.

Like every other one of the thousands—perhaps ten thousand—Saudi princes and princesses, Latifa and Turki supported their lifestyle almost wholly out of the stipend that they received from the Treasury every year. Even small children receive this income: It is calculated by age, ranking in power, and gender. Girls receive half the share of boys. In addition, all public utilities are free for princes.

This is the Saudi system—an accumulation of more and more people into a royal family that treats the country's oil wealth as its personal treasury. Abdel Aziz ibn Saud, the first King, who created Saudi Arabia out of the desert, had at least seventeen wives. When he died in 1953, he left behind forty-four sons. (I don't think anyone knows how many daughters he had. Even the number of his wives is a matter of speculation.) Before he died, Abdel Aziz laid out the succession. Saud, the oldest son, would follow Abdel Aziz as King, and would be assisted by the second oldest son, Faisal. As in all the great Saudi families, the oldest brother took control over the clan.

But King Saud was a disaster. He was a spendthrift, self-indulgent and petty where Abdel Aziz had been austere and cunning. By 1958, dissatisfaction with Saud's rule led a group of important princes and religious leaders to step in. Faisal, the Crown Prince, ruled the country in Saud's name for two years, but Faisal tried to limit the royal family's outrageous spending, and Saud returned to control in 1960. But after a few more years of Saud's rule, the country was veering on the edge of financial disaster. In 1964, the religious leadership issued a ruling that Saud was unfit to govern the country. Faisal was named King; Saud went into exile, and lived in Europe until he died in 1969.

King Faisal was a moderate, dignified man, and his rule is generally seen as having improved the country immensely. He sought to limit the princes' abuse of their position. But in March 1975 King Faisal was shot by one of his nephews, an Islamic radical.

Abdel Aziz had set the pattern of succession: Power went from his oldest son to his second son. The logical next step, therefore, would have been to install Abdel Aziz's third son on the throne. That would have been Prince Mohamed—a violent and fiercely conservative man who would later become infamous as the man who ordered his young granddaughter Princess Mish'al put to death.

It is said that the royal family feared that war or rebellion would break out if Prince Mohamed took the throne. For whatever reason, Prince Mohamed was persuaded to step aside from the succession. Khaled, the fourth son of Abdel Aziz, became King on Faisal's death.

King Khaled was rather mild and paternal—and popular:

His reign coincided with Saudi Arabia's boom years. When he died of a heart attack in 1982, he was succeeded by his brother, Crown Prince Fahd. Fahd was not the next son in line, but the royal family seems to have concluded that he would be the most suitable candidate.

Weakened by multiple health problems, King Fahd remains on the throne to this day. Fahd is likely to be succeeded by his brother Abdallah, who is now over seventy. But nothing is definite: The succession is not clearly defined by law, but is the result of consultations and intrigue in secret councils of the royal family and religious leadership. It is said that King Fahd (or his clan) opposes Abdallah, who is deeply conservative and has criticized the loose morals and high living of his family. The infighting is said to be intense. It is a strange kind of nonsystem, and the uncertainty of the succession keeps an enormous crowd of courtiers buzzing with power struggles and rumors.

Naturally, the Bin Laden clan is prominent among those courtiers. Salem is dead now—he died in a flying accident in Texas in 1988—and his rule over the family has passed to his brother Bakr. Bakr is allied to King Fahd's favorite son, Abdel Aziz. To Yeslam's irritation, Bakr is now privileged among the privileged, at court.

Sometime in 1994, just before our divorce procedure began, Yeslam confided in me that King Fahd was growing unwell. He said that conservatives were likely to take over. Osama, who had been forced to leave Saudi Arabia after he publicly condemned the decadent living of some of the Saudi princes, had gone into exile in Sudan, Yeslam told me. He had a group of armed followers and tanks that guarded his compound. Soon, Yeslam implied, it would be Osama's star that rose over the Bin Laden family. Then Bakr would see what he would see.

That was before Osama's name was linked to a series of terrorist attacks on Saudi Arabia and the West. I know nothing of the Saudi royal family's view of Osama Bin Laden today. But I know that to this day, no Saudi prince or member of the Bin Laden family has acknowledged that Osama directed the attacks on the Twin Towers.

To date, the King of Saudi Arabia has always been one after another of the aging sons of Abdel Aziz, who founded the country. None of his grandsons has yet taken over the throne—which may be one reason why Saudi Arabia never changes. The family keeps growing: Latifa told me there was always at least one al-Saud child born every month—great- and great-great grandchildren now. By the time I lived in Saudi Arabia, there were well over five thousand princes in the royal family. Some say the al-Sauds now number over twenty-five thousand.

When Abdel Aziz ibn Saud named himself King in 1932, Saudi Arabia was desperately poor. His first palace was made of the same sun-dried mud-bricks that the peasants used. In those days, sheikhs and Bedouin herdsmen called each other by their first names. But then oil was discovered in the 1930s.

Since this was Abdel Aziz's country—it was even named after him—it was, I suppose, considered natural that the oil wealth go principally to his children. By the time I lived there, every member of the colossal al-Saud family received enough money to live on quite well.

But in addition, a large number of princes—those who were closest to the crown, or simply the most venal—skimmed huge percentages off major business contracts, for everything from cleaning the roads to renovating an airport or purchasing modern weapons. They lived in unbelievable extravagance. Oil was their personal harvest.

The princely practice of skimming percentages—which, to call a spade a spade, is corruption—was not considered immoral by any Saudi I ever met. Yet at the same time, it was *haram* to gain interest from a savings account, because the Koran forbids the practice of usury. I couldn't understand contradictions like this. Still, I did sometimes find them comical. One time, Yeslam's brother Tareg owed some bank a considerable sum of money. He refused to pay the interest, claiming it would be un-Islamic, and as far as I know nobody ever made him do it.

However, many princes were not in the high spheres of power, and their stipend didn't even approach the millions of dollars of annual income reserved for the King's brothers and sons. Often, to supplement that income, they would open their own businesses, as the commoners did. Small contracting, fashion boutiques, interior design. Decorators were flying into Jeddah by the dozens in those days. Everyone was redoing their houses, in a kind of frenzy—knowing that they should, because everyone else was, but not quite knowing how.

There was a fierce kind of competition about such houses: Huge luxury mansions, the most glamorous that money could buy, would be topped six months later by even huger, grander versions. There was marble everywhere in these homes, halls as big as a hotel lobby, gaudy chandeliers—it was like walking into a furniture store, with no harmony, everything oversized and ill-matched.

Latifa and I would meet, talk, lend each other videocassettes. We went on shopping trips: One time, she was amused when she and Yeslam urged me to buy a beautifully embroidered haute couture dress at Chanel, in Paris, and I said I just couldn't bear to spend $60,000 on something that in Saudi Arabia I could only wear once. Latifa and I cried together at *Sophie's Choice*. We talked about our husbands. And often, I would still be sitting in her living room when her relatives came to visit, as the afternoon drew to an end.

Some of the Saudi princesses whom I met then, and later, lived lives of such decadence and inertia that it was hard not to feel disgust. They were brought up in complete obedience and absolute foolishness. Some were married to men who had several wives, and they had very little to do with their husbands. A few had been divorced. Their children were cared for by battalions of maids and household personnel, and though those princesses lacked for nothing in terms of material possessions, they also had nothing to do.

As the Queens of France did in the olden days, the princesses lived in separate houses alongside the houses of their husbands. The women's houses were smaller, with a separate women's gate; the two houses might share a kitchen, or one set of kitchen staff, but otherwise they had two separate armies of servants—only women servants on the women's side. Their drivers were male, but they were always accompanied if they went out—they were never alone with their drivers. The only men these women ever saw were their husbands, and perhaps their fathers and brothers, or sons.

The princesses would get up sometime in the mid-afternoon, get dressed, make phone calls, perhaps play with their children. Then they could go shopping. Shopping can be a consolation for many ills, and it was a major activity for the princesses. By this time, there were expensive, women's-only shops, with female Lebanese or Egyptian shop assistants, and you could actually see the clothes you were choosing without a black veil over your eyes.

Inside their own homes they were free to wear Yves Saint Laurent miniskirts, outrageous makeup, and plunging necklines. Inside their homes, they were free to do more or less what they liked. But they were prisoners. Outside, they were completely shrouded, as I was, in the abaya. It was like carrying a jail on your back.

By the early 1980s, there were a few restaurants in Saudi Arabia. One or two had initiated "family" sections, where a man and wife could sit with their children—the wife trying to eat while fully veiled, attempting to expose not one inch of skin while forking spaghetti into her mouth. Some restaurants also had women's sections, where you could take your veil off, and the waiter would knock before entering: You quickly veiled for every change of plate or fresh bottle of Perrier. So there was this activity for them, too: a strange, sad little version of a restaurant.

At dusk, the princesses would visit each other, or prepare for dinner—a women-only dinner. Often you could hear the dinner going on in the adjoining, husband's house. The wife might even phone her husband, a few yards away, to advise him to serve this or that delicacy. Conversation was mostly about clothes, or gossip. The ignorance of these women was abyssal: It was as if they'd never been to school. (Their children, too, were ignorant: No teacher could discipline a young princeling.) The food was never very good, but it was abundant: great stews with beans and rice, and ornate baskets of fruit that tasted of nothing.

Many of the princesses lived on pills—prescription, naturally. They made a beeline for the chic doctors on Harley Street every time they went to London, checking into clinics for countless tests. Some owned gym rooms and had their own indoor swimming pools, but nobody ever swam that I could see. These women never saw the light of day.

They had bone density problems from the lack of sunlight and exercise, heart problems from eating too much, psychosomatic problems galore. A very large proportion of these women were depressed. They lived alongside husbands who had almost nothing to do with them and in the constant fear that they might one day be divorced. They had no responsibility, and no control of anything. They lived in complete dependence, in a kind of waking slumber. It was no kind of life.

If I had had no other aspirations for the future of my daughters perhaps I could have accepted that life for them, and we would be among them still.

There is such emotional emptiness in Saudi Arabia. People need human contact. They need approval, and love, and a sense of shared thoughts. But these women, so cut off from the world, seemed to have no real link with their husbands. Segregated since birth, they could not establish any kind of true contact with the opposite sex.

Perhaps as a result, some of the princesses had affairs with each other. They would fall passionately in love, become jealous, stage enormous sulks. It mostly struck me as sad. It's one thing if you're born a lesbian; it's quite another if you're taking refuge there because you're married to a man who spends no time with you, and with whom you have next to nothing to share.

We had all heard rumors of a kind of lesbian party circuit in Riyadh, where women would socialize and pick each other up. I knew of one Egyptian woman married to a high-placed Saudi who fell in love with a princess. She was miserable when the princess left her. Probably in Riyadh they had rumors of such a circuit in Jeddah. I never actually saw these parties myself, but I was propositioned once. It was all too strange for me.

Most of the men probably didn't know their wives were sleeping with other women. But those who did learn of it may not have cared enough to want to stop them. Women don't matter to a Saudi man. Possessing them matters—matters crucially—but once the women are locked in and breeding, what happens among them doesn't count for much.

Homosexuality is forbidden in Saudi Arabia—punished by public flogging. But many men have homosexual relationships, especially when they're young, before they're married. If two men hold hands in the street, as they often do, it's not seen as sexual, but if a man and a woman do the same—even if they're married—it's perceived as obscene, people are appalled, and the religious police surge up with batons.

The habit of teenage homosexuality doesn't always go away as men age, and in that respect the al-Saud princes are like everyone else—except perhaps more so. You hear rumors. A European decorator I once met told me he thought there were more gay men in Saudi Arabia than in Europe.

One Saudi man we knew well—and whose wife we knew well, too—once turned up at our house in Switzerland with a very gay German man sitting beside him in his blue Porsche. I didn't know what, if anything, they did together. I wouldn't have minded. People should do as they wish. But I knew this same man would never have turned up at our house with a woman who was not his wife. The hypocrisy of that way of living really got to me.

I didn't meet many of the al-Saud princes. I know that these women did have their male equivalents, who lived lives of waste, ignorance, and debauchery. You hear about them often enough in the West. I heard the rumors of planeloads of call girls flying in for the weekend from Paris. I'm not sure these rumors are true—you would have a lot of trouble getting visas and authorizations at the airport for a crew like that, unless you were very highly placed. If such parties did happen in Jeddah, then Yeslam never told me about them.

But I did hear about such antics when princes were hospitalized in Geneva, in detox clinics, for heroin or alcohol, or cocaine. And, like everyone, I heard about the obscenely lavish sex parties in Europe.

In the summer, when the al-Saud court dispersed throughout Europe, Yeslam would often meet with Prince Majid, and later Prince Meshal, in Geneva. When he brought them home, I would retire upstairs: Our guests were of that old school. They may not have worked very hard, but they had a dignified aura. Their faith was unshakable and they had a profound attachment to Bedouin culture.

One time, I was walking through Geneva, shopping, in a knee-length dress, when I caught sight of Yeslam and Prince Meshal on the other side of the road. Yeslam crossed over to talk to me, but Prince Meshal stayed where he was, and looked away slightly. Even in Switzerland, he wouldn't look at another Saudi man's wife.

When I was abroad, I was free. I certainly wanted nothing to do with the al-Saud protocol when I was in Europe. I suppose Yeslam probably would have liked me to pay court to the wives and retinues of the princes, who often rented whole floors of the best hotels in town. I gave them as little attention as possible, but occasionally I felt obliged to pay a visit. It was like being transported to Jeddah. Sometimes one entire floor of one of the Geneva luxury hotels would be reborn as a Saudi women's quarter. Stepping out of the elevator, you would find the Jeddah servants, the pungent Jeddah incense, and the Jeddah patterns of behavior.

Once, at a dinner party at the Saudi embassy in Geneva, I was seated beside the daughter of one of the princes—a flashy, overbearing woman. She launched into a story about King Faisal, who supposedly told her he had seen one man cause another to levitate into the air. I turned and said—not in an insulting tone—"I don't believe you." She was so outraged to be challenged that she swiveled in her chair and didn't address another word to me all evening. Like so many Saudi royals, she couldn't tolerate contradiction—especially from a foreigner.

I had no desire to be at the beck and call of these women, accompanying them on their outrageous shopping trips, dressed like masked creatures from another planet. Wherever they went, they transported the Kingdom with them—and I didn't want to be there. Switzerland was where I could be myself. For those blessed few weeks every summer, I clung to my own life. I wanted nothing to do with the Saudi Arabian way of life.

CHAPTER 18

Leaving Saudi Arabia

YESLAM'S PERSONAL BUSINESS WAS FLOURISHING, AS
was the Bin Laden Organization. Everyone in Saudi
Arabia seemed to be making money, with building projects
on a pharaonic scale springing out of the sand almost daily.
For three years, Yeslam had the only brokerage in Saudi
Arabia, and the great merchant families, as well as many
Bin Laden brothers, took their money to him for investment. (At the time, most of the Saudi princes didn't invest
with Yeslam—they didn't want another Saudi to know how
much they were really worth.)

But Yeslam continued to complain of his ailments. He
was irritable and selfish. My husband was becoming more
childish and demanding, more centered on himself and his
more or less imaginary illnesses. He refused to believe the
doctors, who maintained that he was in perfect health, and
was becoming increasingly detached from legitimate con-
cerns such as the children's needs.

In the beginning, I'd always seen Yeslam's Saudi nationality as a minor detail; but now he was slowly becoming more

deeply Saudi. He was imposing Saudi culture on us. The girls were growing, and Yeslam was becoming more critical of their behavior, and he seemed to want them to be more modest in the way they dressed.

Yeslam snapped at the children for wearing tight clothes or short-shorts, insisting that they change before we went out—even in Geneva. He had always left me in sole charge of the girls, but now I felt that he no longer trusted my judgment. It seemed like the well-being of our daughters didn't interest him.

As Yeslam was becoming more Saudi, Saudi Arabia was becoming more schizophrenic. The more debauched princes continued indulging in their privately lavish lifestyles, while at the same time the royal family enforced increasing restrictions on the ordinary people they ruled. Extremist ideas were taking hold everywhere.

Some of the Bin Laden sisters began complaining that their children were exposed to too much Western influence. The most narrow-minded sisters-in-law came up with a solution: They would set up their own girls' school in Jeddah, with much stricter Islamic instruction. They invited me to register Wafah and Najia there. Many of the other sisters-in-law registered their children.

Once, I would have scoffed at the idea, or attempted a passionate discussion with my sisters-in-law to explain why I thought they were wrong. Now, I merely smiled and murmured that my children were happy where they were. I could no longer bear to stick my neck out. It was useless. My hopes for real change were by now completely shattered. Nobody—not even Yeslam—would have understood how horrifying I found the idea of sending my little girls to an even more restrictive school.

Only a handful of the cousins attended my children's birthday party that year. I suppose my sisters-in-law could no longer tolerate the music and dancing. In their view, my girls were approaching puberty, and they should be behaving more like future Saudi women than foolish Western girls.

Yeslam and I had fallen into a routine of spending all of the children's vacations in our house in Switzerland. It became our real home, for good, in 1985. That summer the power struggles intensified and Yeslam complained endlessly of ailments as usual—his lungs were weak, his heart was not strong, his stomach pained him. When September came around, and it was time to return for Jeddah for the start of the school term, I found Yeslam still hadn't made any plane reservations. He said he felt too unwell.

The days crept past. I was only too relieved to scratch a few extra days of summer freedom out of the grim, bleak school year in Jeddah, but by the end of September the children were restive. I told Yeslam that they had to attend school somewhere. If he hadn't made plane reservations by mid-October, I would have to register them at school in Geneva.

I held my breath. By October 15, Yeslam still hadn't taken any action. I quietly drove to an international school outside Geneva. It was like a dream—computer labs, language labs, sports facilities, art classes. The school was mixed. Most of the children were from families who worked at the United Nations, and they were bright, joyful, unafraid. I spoke with the principal, explained the situation, registered Wafah and

Najia for the semester. Then I went home, and told Yeslam that I had made temporary arrangements for the girls to attend school.

Their first day, they wore jeans, like everyone else. They came home bursting with information. There were boys in the classroom! There were no classes in religion, no more hours of learning the Koran by heart; there were debates! Girls played sports—they could play tennis, and soccer! They could join music classes, a drama club! They were far behind for their age—in French, and grammar, of course, but also in math and geography—but they were thrilled. And so was I.

I tried to caution myself against too much joy—this was too good to last. It would all change when Yeslam decided to take us back to Jeddah, and returning home would be even harder for the girls after they had lived through such freedom. Still, inwardly, I was jubilant.

In November, Mikhail Gorbachev and Ronald Reagan had a historic summit meeting in Switzerland. Our village, located just outside Geneva, bristled with army trucks, with multiple checkpoints on the road, and the threatening atmosphere panicked Yeslam. He said we should leave—said it was too dangerous to stay. I knew full well that our village was probably the safest place on the planet at that point, since the President of the United States was staying there, but there was no reasoning with Yeslam's alarm. He wanted us all to go to London for the summit's duration.

The children had just started school; I felt it was unfair to pull them out so quickly. And I didn't want to establish a precedent—I so longed for them to spend one entire, blissful semester in Switzerland. So, to pacify Yeslam, who refused to take the plane on his own, I agreed to leave for London with him, and arranged for a tutor to come and look after the girls for a few days, along with my dear Dita, our faithful Filipina nanny.

It was only when I was seated in the plane that I realized that Yeslam, who was persuaded that our house was in danger, had let the children stay there. I knew it was safe. But Yeslam believed that it wasn't—and nonetheless he had left the children there. According to his logic, he had abandoned them. I swiveled and examined Yeslam as he sat beside me. The day we really are in danger, I thought, will Yeslam be the first to leave? Does he no longer care for anyone but himself?

Yeslam could still function, at least professionally. He already had a company with an office in Geneva. Now he began meeting the Saudi princes as they arrived in Geneva for vacations, cultivating them as friends and clients, becoming a kind of right-hand man. Yeslam knew people at the Saudi embassy and at Saudia, the national airline, and they kept him informed of who was scheduled to come to town. Yeslam would greet the princes at the airport and spend afternoons and evenings with them. Among them was Prince Meshal, one of the great Saudi princes, a brother of King Khaled and his successor, King Fahd.

Yeslam was always crazy about clothes and must have owned over three hundred suits. Now he went into overdrive. He developed a kind of competition with Prince Meshal as to who would be the most elegant. Yeslam always said King Fahd would pay any expense Prince Meshal could incur, because Fahd wanted to keep Meshal out of the succession, despite his rank. By age, Meshal should be the successor to the Sultan; but Fahd had other plans for the Kingdom, Yeslam told me. This was the price King Fahd was willing to pay: He bought Meshal's birthright to take over the throne.

I was so thrilled at the children's progress in school. They were so happy, and as their first semester ended, their teachers informed us that they were catching up quickly with the curriculum. But I felt despondent and utterly overcome by Yeslam's erratic behavior

Little by little, I had begun to feel alone with my husband. Even when he was physically present, Yeslam seemed not to be emotionally engaged. Simple pleasures—watching the children play, or swimming with them, or reading—no longer held his interest. With me, Yeslam complained constantly of feeling unwell, and talked of little other than his ailments and his family problems. He seemed to feel well, and sharp, only in the company of the Saudi princes.

I was simply too exhausted to carry a whole family without help. I wanted to shake him out of this funk he was in. I worried for Yeslam—I felt he needed professional help and yet I couldn't seem to help him. It's hard seeing someone complain of symptoms that seem imaginary. Often we would dress for an outing and begin driving into town only to stop and turn back—Yeslam couldn't face it.

Paradoxically, Yeslam was becoming more Saudi now that we were in Europe. In Saudi Arabia, he and I had shared our bewilderment at Saudi society and socialized with Westerners. Now, living in a modern society, Yeslam sought out the company of other Saudi men, expectantly awaiting the arrival of the princes. He seemed to need his roots, and with me and the children he became far more domineering.

I was living in the free world now, but I found that I must always be at Yeslam's disposal. I never went out socially without him; he even accompanied me to lunches with women friends. In a closed society, Yeslam gave me small freedoms; but now, in an open society, he clenched shut.

I don't know if it was the influence of the Saudi men he socialized with, but Yeslam began seeing other women. One spring day the phone rang. A man said, "Tell your husband to stop running after my wife." It was the husband of Yeslam's secretary. I was devastated. I had thought Yeslam was out late at night with the princes. He didn't have many male friends, so when he went out without me I just assumed it was always for business. I realized he had been lying to me. I was shaken.

Yeslam told me I was hysterical. At first he stonewalled, insisted he had done nothing. When I threatened to leave, he panicked. We made up, eventually, but something truly was wrong with our marriage.

I became pregnant once more. I knew that I would have this child, no matter what: This child was God-sent. When Yeslam dared to ask me to have another abortion, I felt disgust with him. How could he ask me to repeat that horrible procedure and its long, sad aftermath? Never, I told him. No matter what. Never again.

With hindsight, I suppose this was when Yeslam finally felt I let him down. I went ahead with the pregnancy, though he had asked me not to. This was the end of my marriage: my refusal, his anger.

But perhaps the long, sad process that led to the end of my marriage had begun far earlier, in Saudi Arabia, when Yeslam's bold, Western personality began to crack and unravel. Perhaps it was the constant tension among the brothers, and their hidden struggle for money, power, and prestige, that undid my husband. After the Mecca revolt, nothing in Saudi Arabia was ever the same. It was then, I think, that the tensions between fundamentalist extremism and Western-generated ideas of material wealth became unbearable; then, that Saudi Arabia began in some sense to realize that its culture was splitting into a modern economy and an ancient social code—contradictions that Saudi culture was unable, or unwilling, to resolve. Perhaps it was that tension that gnawed away at Yeslam, too.

Or perhaps it was when Yeslam and I left Saudi Arabia. Living in a foreign country with his family, as he aged, his roots tugged at him.

Whatever the cause—whatever the moment when the wind finally shifted course—Yeslam had changed. All through my pregnancy, he barely spoke to me. He was cold, silent, forbidding. He would come back late, at three or four in the morning. My husband was truly a stranger to me then.

When the baby was born, I named her Noor—the light. And she was indeed my light, later, when the world around me sometimes seemed so dark. Even just hours old, Noor was so lovely, with her huge open eyes—never wrinkled and red like most babies are, but calm, from the beginning, and clear-sighted.

Yeslam made efforts to be attentive after Noor's birth; he was affectionate with her, and even with me. He insisted I return home from the clinic early, and I did. I had to leave Noor there, because she had a mild case of jaundice. Yeslam accompanied me to the clinic at least once a day to feed her.

Part of me tried to persuade myself that Yeslam was happy. But more likely he already knew then that everything would be over soon; more likely he was happy because he had someone else. I understood that something had been broken between us, but I didn't know what to do to make it mend. I spent hours on the phone with Mary Martha, seeking comfort.

Noor was born in April 1987. In September, I saw Yeslam with another woman. I hadn't been able to sleep that night, and as I often did, I took the car out for a drive around town. (For some reason cars have always soothed me.) As I happened to drive past Yeslam's offices downtown, I caught sight of his car. So I parked and waited. It was about one in the morning when Yeslam walked out, with a woman.

I confronted him. Yeslam denied that he knew the woman, but he was obviously lying. I knew then that I should leave him, but I couldn't bear to hurt the children. And above all, I feared that he would try to take them away from me—take them back to Saudi Arabia. Worn out by Noor's recent birth and the loneliness of my pregnancy, I was exhausted and depressed—I couldn't face the battle that I knew would lie ahead.

Meanwhile, Yeslam had begun pressuring me to sign a legal agreement. It was a sort of prenuptial agreement, except that it was post-nuptial. Yeslam told me it was a formality, to protect the children's security. My doctor advised me that I was in no state to make any big decisions, but when I hesitated, Yeslam became grimmer than I had ever seen him.

"Look, I didn't want Noor, and you went ahead anyway," he told me. "If you don't want problems—if you want me to accept her—you'll trust me, and you'll sign it."

I was a wreck, physically and mentally. Yeslam threatened me. He said, again and again, that he would take the girls to Jeddah and leave them with his mother. I could not bear his constant pressure. I knew that under Swiss law Yeslam would be allowed to take the children on vacation, alone. And I knew that if the children ever set foot in Saudi Arabia, I would never see them again. No government on earth would ever get them out.

I felt trapped, by my own husband. The only thing that mattered to me was that he not touch my daughters. At my wit's end and in a state of panic, I gave in, and signed that paper, out of fear and for the sake of peace. More than anything, I needed to end Yeslam's harassment.

Things only got worse after I signed the document, though. Yeslam didn't change, as I had hoped he would. He was increasingly distant; he was rarely at home. My own health worsened. I began losing weight—I couldn't eat. I could barely look after the children. I was hospitalized for a few days in October, hooked up to intravenous feeding tubes. I weighed ninety-nine pounds.

That Christmas, struggling to maintain a semblance of normal family life for the girls, I took baby Noor and the children to the mountains. Yeslam was supposed to meet us there, but he called and said that Prince Meshal was in town. Part of me wanted to believe him, but I knew he was lying.

On New Year's Eve, Yeslam went out, but came home early. He fell asleep—we had begun sleeping in separate bedrooms. The phone kept ringing, but every time I answered the caller hung up. I woke him, told him I thought someone was trying to call. The next morning he went out early and came back claiming it had probably all been a stupid, drunken New Year's joke.

I was vulnerable, but I was not an imbecile. I might have reacted differently if Yeslam had been honest with me, but I couldn't accept such blatant lies. We had an argument. Yeslam was livid. I asked him to leave. He slammed the door, and he left.

So, on New Year's Day of 1988, my life changed.

What followed was bitter, and draining, and I see little benefit to dwelling on it. The girls and I remained in Switzerland. The Bin Laden family rejected them completely. Once, I went to visit Yeslam's brother Ibrahim, who had been my friend, and pleaded for him to intercede with Yeslam. But Ibrahim told me, "No matter how right you are, Carmen, my brother is never wrong."

Another time, Najia caught sight of Om Yeslam—her grandmother—and Fawzia, her aunt, on a street in Geneva. These women turned away from my little girl, who had grown up in their company. None of the Bin Ladens, even those who seemed to enjoy my company, ever had the strength of mind to stand up to Yeslam and contact me, or the children who had grown up at their side.

Our divorce proceedings have been appalling. Yeslam has poured all his might and money into a colossal effort to keep me under his control, and exact his revenge. Although he had promised not to, he demanded the right to take Noor to Saudi Arabia—not Wafah and Najia, I suppose, because he thought the older children would refuse. He fought every detail tooth and nail. Yeslam dragged the legal procedure out over the longest possible time, so that he could hide his assets and deprive the children and myself of his financial support.

Perhaps the worst moment of our long story together came after I was granted custody of the children. That's when Yeslam claimed that he was not Noor's father. It was unspeakably low of him, and utterly humiliating—to me, and above all to little Noor. It's hard to see how anyone could do such a thing; his claim was of course false, as we proved.

I had to ask that all of us go through DNA tests to confirm that Yeslam was lying, and that Noor really is her father's child. She was just nine years old. We all had to be tested; Yeslam walked into the clinic while Noor and I were in the doctor's office. Wafah sprang at him, and asked how he could do something like that. Yeslam just ignored her. He walked straight past his daughters.

From that day on, Yeslam never spoke again to any of his daughters, or to me.

The whole battle continues to this day. We are legally separated; Wafah and Najia are legally adults and Noor is safe in my custody. But I attempt to support us all on alimony payments allotted me by a Swiss court, which amount to less than the monthly salary of Yeslam's private pilot. Sometimes I feel like David, to Yeslam's Goliath.

If we had been in Saudi Arabia, the divorce would have been so simple for Yeslam. It would have been over in less than half a day, and I would have lost my children forever. But we were in Switzerland. And one man believed in the threat that hung over my daughters—my Swiss lawyer, Frédéric Marti.

Yeslam lives in Geneva now, as I do. When he sees his daughters, he stares right through them. He refuses any contact with them whatsoever, and when Wafah was accepted to Columbia Law School, in New York, he said he would never support her, because there was no point in her studying more.

Yeslam asked for Swiss nationality in the late 1990s, which provoked great controversy in Switzerland. But early in 2001—for whatever reason—obtaining a Swiss passport seemed suddenly to become very important and urgent to him. So Yeslam staged an elaborate media campaign, claiming that he needed to be sure he could live in Switzerland in order to maintain close relations with his children—even though in reality he had completely cut off contact with them for many years. I cannot help thinking he used our children to further his interests. However, in May 2001, Yeslam was rewarded with his Swiss passport.

But whatever his official nationality, by now Yeslam is truly a Saudi.

He has ceaselessly harassed us with legal procedures. Twice I received frightening official letters from Saudi Arabia demanding that I appear before a court of law in Jeddah. When my lawyer asked for an explanation, Yeslam claimed that this was for a Saudi divorce. But I knew that he was lying—a Saudi divorce doesn't require the presence of the wife. I believe that Yeslam charged me with adultery.

In Saudi Arabia, the sentence for that would be death.

If he has charged me with adultery, as I believe he has, then Yeslam has cut me off not only from Saudi Arabia but from the entire Middle East. I am afraid to set foot in any Muslim countries that have close legal ties with Saudi Arabia because I could be extradited; and I would be at the mercy of a legal system that would be prepared to carry out a death sentence on an innocent woman. I fear for my life.

I have come to believe that dealing with my unbelievably lengthy divorce is the price that I will have to pay for my daughters' freedom. Although it has been a long and bitter fight, it is not such a very high price to pay for the precious knowledge that my three girls can now live as they wish.

Yeslam's rejection of our daughters hurt them enormously as they grew up. They still pay a heavy emotional price. Rejection—especially a father's rejection—is a very hard thing for a little girl to have to bear. A father's admiration and love is so important; I know a little of what it is like. I felt that awful grief and guilt myself, as a child, when my own father left us. I, too, suffered, as have my daughters; I, too, felt myself painfully to blame. It is a terrible thing to watch this happen to my children.

I wonder, now, if Yeslam cut off his daughters because Saudi values are foreign to them. They are intelligent, educated, beautiful, lively, and graceful; they are free women. But perhaps he only really sees them as pawns—tools that he can use against me. Or maybe as enemies. Perhaps to him they seem unworthy of his attention, because they are Western women, willful and independent.

My struggle to keep my daughters has made me stronger. But it seems to me that Yeslam has changed far more than I have. Or perhaps my husband was always cruel, self-centered, arrogant, dismissive: His Saudi background simply caught up with him as he grew older. I was blind to reality, starstruck and foolish, imagining a love story where there was only a struggle for power and dominance. Once I disobeyed, my dream turned to dust, and my charming prince turned against me: It was all a Saudi fairy tale, and the brunt of my punishment will always be borne by my children.

Wafah and Najia are adults now. Noor is getting older, too. We have decided to keep our name—Yeslam's name. Whatever has happened between us, Yeslam remains my children's father. And our name is Bin Ladin. Once, it was a name like any other. Today it has become a synonym of blind violence and terror. We could of course try to change our name. But my daughters and I have nothing to hide, and we do not want to mislead anyone. The truth always catches up with you one day, and changing our name would not change who we are.

If my daughters go back to Saudi Arabia one day, it will be their free choice—as, long ago, it was mine. But, as a mother, I hope with every fiber of my body they never do.

CHAPTER 19

Conclusion

FOR MANY PEOPLE, SEPTEMBER 11, 2001, MARKED the start of a new era. Thousands of innocent people lost their lives, and countless more were irreparably damaged. It was a wake-up call. That day opened the eyes of the West to a vast and powerful menace of which few had been aware. For the first time, the Western world had to measure the power of Islamic fundamentalism to rock its foundations. Osama Bin Laden and his followers—who number in the thousands—were able to take our freedom hostage.

The World Trade Center attack robbed us all of a certain innocence. No one will ever be able to take an airplane again without a sense of apprehension. We are no longer safe. Nobody can truly feel secure now, and certainly not my daughters and myself.

I have lived in the Bin Laden clan; I have analyzed the workings of Saudi society. And I fear for the future of the free world. My fear—and outrage—is based on my conviction that a large majority of Saudis support the extremist ideas of Osama Bin Laden, and that the Bin Ladens and the

Saudi royal family continue to operate hand in hand, even if their relations are sometimes too intricate for their convergent convictions to be apparent.

I cannot believe that the Bin Ladens have cut Osama off completely. I simply can't see them depriving a brother of his annual dividend from their father's company, and sharing it among themselves. This would be unthinkable—among the Bin Ladens, no matter what a brother does, he remains a brother.

It's certainly possible that Osama retains ties to the royal family, too. The Bin Ladens and the princes work together, very closely. They are secretive, and they are united. They have been inextricably linked for many decades through close friendships and business ventures. Most of the Bin Laden brothers have business partnerships and direct vested interests with at least one Saudi prince (for example Bakr Bin Laden is a business associate of Abdel Aziz Ben Fahd, the King's preferred son; Yeslam Bin Laden, my former husband, has privileged links with Prince Meshal Ben Abdel Aziz).

Both clans want us to believe that they have no connection whatsoever with Osama Bin Laden and the barbaric acts that led to 9/11. Though they have made few public statements condemning the tragedy, neither clan has gone to any length to prove that they have not given Osama Bin Laden and Al Qaida moral and financial support in the past, and that they are not currently doing so.

I openly defy the Saudi ruling class—the Bin Ladens and the Saudi royal family—to open their books and prove to the world where they stand. In the current precarious political climate, no one can afford to hide behind the weak excuse of privacy. I believe it is the duty of each and every one of us to do everything in our power to fight against terrorism.

These are people who feel contempt for the outside world. Individually, some may claim to be liberal. But the beliefs and ideology of their culture are deeply ingrained in them from an early age—they are inescapable.

Saudis don't openly argue with each other. Sometimes the thirst for power, greed, and material interests might separate the brothers in a family like the al-Sauds, or the Bin Ladens. But they are always brought back together by the bonds of their shared beliefs and religious convictions, and their upbringing.

Osama Bin Laden and those like him didn't spring, fully formed, from the desert sand. They were made. They were fashioned by the workings of an opaque and intolerant medieval society that is closed to the outside world. It is a society where half the population have had their basic rights as people amputated, and obedience to the strictest rules of Islam must be absolute.

Despite all the power of their oil revenue, the Saudis are structured by a hateful, backward-looking view of religion, and an education that is a school for intolerance. They learn scorn for what is foreign: The non-Muslim doesn't count. Their mothers spoil them into arrogance. But then their every natural urge is denied by endless, oppressive restrictions. Obedience to the patriarch is absolute. And when they become fathers, their rule is law.

When Osama dies, I fear there will be a thousand men to take his place. The ground of Saudi Arabia is fertile soil for intolerance and arrogance, and for contempt toward outsiders. It is a country where there is no room for mildness, mercy, compassion, or doubt. Every detail of life is defined absolutely. Every inclination for natural pleasure and emotion is forbidden. Saudis have the unshakable conviction that they are right. They head the Islamic nations. They were born in the land of Mecca. Their way has been chosen by God.

I have never yet met a Saudi who truly admires our Western society. They don't necessarily seem overtly hostile (though they are often condescending and arrogant). They are eager to use our technology, and they understand our political systems. But inside them, there is nothing but scorn for what they perceive as the godless, individualistic values and shameless freedoms of the Western way of life.

And yet, in Saudi Arabia there is much drug abuse and promiscuity. There is homosexuality, and AIDS. And there is certainly much more hypocrisy than anywhere in the West that I have ever been. But these things are not openly displayed, or honestly discussed. For the Saudis, it seems, what is hidden does not exist.

There must be geniuses lost in that people. Osama, perhaps, could have been one. But though he lived in the twenty-first century, he did not use his might and power to bring people closer together—to promote goodwill and tolerance. Instead, he chose discord and destruction.

In the end, I believe that what shaped Osama is the strict Wahabi doctrine. In my analysis and experience, a vast majority of people in Saudi Arabia feel just like him. In their eyes, you cannot be too religious. They have no room to grow as individuals. They are desperately angry at the West for its countless, irresistible temptations. They refuse to evolve, to adapt. For them, it is easier to crush those temptations—to destroy them, to kill them, like an errant teenager. I hope I am wrong but, unfortunately, I believe that the fundamentalists who are at the receiving end of Saudi Arabia's oil wealth are here to stay. I fear that if we, in the Western world, are not vigilant enough, there will be no end to their terrorism. They will use our tolerance to infiltrate our society with their intolerance.

In those long years I spent in Saudi Arabia, and the years of struggle that followed, I fought to stay true to myself and to give my daughters what is priceless: freedom of thought. I hope I made the right choice. I don't know if that's as important to them as it is to me. I suppose when I was younger I, too, found it less important. But when I felt it being taken away from me—when I feared that it might slip through my fingers—I found that was the one thing I could not tolerate.

I have seen too many women lose everything, even the right to see their children, and who were forced to submit to the rule of their husbands, because they simply had no other choice. And I have seen men torn between their ambition and desires, and their training for self-denial and obedience to their society's traditions.

Sometimes I wonder whether I would have fought the Bin Laden clan less fiercely if I had had only sons. Materially, it was in many ways a pleasant existence. But as much as material things tempt me, there is one thing that matters far more: freedom.

I am aware that because I dare to speak up, a war will be

declared on my daughters and me by the powerful Bin Laden clan and the Saudi establishment. Lawsuits will be filed, our integrity questioned, our credibility discredited. To them it is a crime for us, as women, to aspire to freedom of thought and the protection of our basic rights as human beings.

But we will fight back. Our defense is the defense of truth. Our serenity—our well-being—our most basic sense of security was shattered and buried on September 11, 2001. Now, more than ever, is the time for us to speak up and rise above the lies and duplicity that made the tragedy possible, to try to protect our future.

Despite everything we have gone through and no matter what the future holds for us, I want my daughters to know that I will never regret saying yes to their father. As a young girl, I accepted him and loved him madly. Unfortunately, I found that as a mother and a woman, I could not accept the beliefs and values that were such an important part of him. I want my daughters to know that I am convinced, deep in my heart and conscience, that by giving them my values, I gave them the most valuable gift of all: freedom. For me, there will never be a better reward than to be able to look at my beautiful daughters and say, "Wafah, Najia, Noor, you are free to live the lives you want to live, and above all you are free to be who you want to be."

Postscript

Three and a half years have gone by since the tragic and dreadful events of September 11, 2001, when so many innocent lives were lost. For the victims' families and loved ones the acute sense of loss and pain continues. My heart goes out to them and I only hope that in some way the passing of time can alleviate their suffering.

My daughters live with a daily reminder of that day, for their name has become synonymous with it. Even if one day they marry, their presence will always provoke an echo of hushed whispers and raised eyebrows. If you're born a Bin Ladin, you'll always be a Bin Ladin—I doubt the stigma will ever go away. Wafah, Najia, and Noor have been raised with the taste of freedom—with the ability to live, to function, and to make decisions for themselves, believing that their willpower and actions will guide their successes or failures. As free Western women they should be able to be the masters of their own destiny, and yet, after years of struggle to obtain that their freedom, my girls are trapped in the prison of their name.

In my daily life and my travels with my girls since 9/11, I have witnessed this often. Strolling down Fifth Avenue in Manhattan, Noor, now 17, stopped me, suddenly taken aback. "Mom, what would all these people think of me if they knew my name?" she asked. I realized that she will ask herself that question all her life. The difficulty—the challenge—that my children now face is enormous, making me wonder if they will ever be able to use their intellectual and artistic gifts to pursue their goals and dreams. My wish is that people will understand their burden, and judge them solely on the basis of their talents and abilities.

With *Inside the Kingdom,* I had hoped to lighten that burden. I had hoped that by being honest about our story and our struggle to gain freedom I could erase any suspicions about where our loyalties lie. And indeed, as we meet people in America who have read my book, or seen me in interviews, we find ourselves overwhelmed by their warmth and generosity, their genuine understanding and fellowship, and their ability to go beyond the obstacle of our name. Even just blocks away from the awful physical reminder of the attacks on the Manhattan landscape, it seems that the people we meet truly welcome us. Knowing the greatness of America and the fairness of its people—their willingness to question facts, their ability to perceive and respect individuals, their empathy and warmth—I can say that I am not surprised. I had always known, deep down, that people from the "land of the free" would understand our inextricable dilemma. But I am moved by my daughters' surprise, and I take this opportunity to say that we will always be immensely grateful for this understanding.

So many people have come up to me in the street to tell me how brave I have been and how much they admire me. I find myself completely at a loss to respond. I don't see myself as brave. I am a woman who carried out my duty and responsibility as a mother. I defended my children, and I defended our principles, our love of freedom. True courage belongs to women like those who set up clandestine classrooms in Afghanistan so they could teach little girls to read and write in spite of the very real danger that the Taliban authorities would find them and have them whipped and imprisoned, or worse. That is my standard of courage.

Inside the Kingdom was also my explanation, to my daughters and to the world, of what I perceived in my years of living in Saudi

Arabia. I expected questions, even criticisms, about those views. I never imagined that my personal story, and my long struggle to keep my daughters, would give rise to such interest and so many questions. Not a week passes by without my receiving kind letters of sympathy and understanding, all of them moving, and each of them touching my heart. One lady wrote to me, "You made me cry, you made me laugh, and above all, you made me think." I could not have dreamed of a more valuable prize. This flood of warmth has reinforced my respect for the American spirit. I also received letters that echoed my sad experience. I have always been aware of the situation of mothers, less fortunate than I, whose children are trapped in Saudi Arabia, and wondered how I could help. Now I have decided to create an association, to join our forces and to bring their plight to the attention of the general public.

After years of living with the constant, chilling fear that I might lose my children, I won the most important personal battle: legal custody. And now I am determined not to be dismissed like a repudiated Saudi wife. The divorce procedure in Geneva courts, which has lasted for more than ten years, has been characterized by misleading statements and outright lies. With the habitual Saudi disdain for judicial systems other than their own, officials of the Bin Laden Organization have refused to appear before the Swiss court. In Yeslam's long effort to hide the vast extent of his wealth, legal requests for evidence from the Saudi Arabian authorities were returned unanswered, or with misleading information. So I found myself obliged to begin a private investigation into the holdings of my husband and the Bin Laden family.

The six-year-long investigation that I undertook led me to the discovery of more than a hundred companies, many of them offshore. Since 9/11, some of those companies have been closed down. In response to the many unanswered questions and the gravity of the subject matter, I am currently working on a book that will throw unprecedented new light on the secret business of the Bin Laden empire.

Generally, as I reflect on my years in Saudi Arabia and my current life in Europe, it seems to me that we are experiencing a clash of cultures between our Western ideals and the values and growing might of Islamic fundamentalism. Fundamentalists have always existed. Thirty years ago, the places they come from started to accumulate the potent wealth of petrodollars. Silently, unnoticed by the West, they began distributing their riches through charities, Koranic schools, mosques, and religious institutions, and their power to influence others began to swell. In 1975 only one country's legal system was based on the Islamic Sharia religious code: Saudi Arabia. Since then, Iran, Sudan and other countries have adopted Sharia too, and most Muslim countries around the world face insistent demands from powerful—often Saudi-funded—fundamentalist groups, that they, too, establish this harsh, medieval code.

The fundamentalists' efforts to impose their values on others are not limited to Muslim countries. I see the signs everywhere. Perhaps because of my background, I am more sensitive to them, or more vigilant. In Canada, I am told, Islamic tribunals in cities such as Toronto seek to regulate divorce, custody, and inheritance issues in the Muslim community—and this is tolerated, under the Arbitration Act of the province of Ontario. This troubles me. In France, some public swimming pools have instituted women-only hours. Throughout Europe, Islamic authorities influence Muslim children to go to school in veils. Girls are deprived of the pleasure of sports, hindered by their veils and cumbersome clothing, and they submit to the strictest form of Islam without speaking out or questioning anything. I find this intolerable. On November 2, 2004, a fanatical fundamentalist assassinated the Dutch filmmaker Theo van Gogh as he strolled through the streets of Amsterdam because he had photographed verses from the Koran printed on women's bodies. I can understand that those images might have shocked some people, but Van Gogh paid with his life for exercising his right to free speech in a democracy. That frightens me.

I frequently find myself in situations that illuminate the unbridgeable gulf between our societies. A few months ago, I was a guest speaker at the Oxford Union debating society. After dinner, the cook asked to speak with me. I listened as he told me that I was giving the West a false picture of Islam. He said he had lived in Britain for years, and had become British. He was a practicing Muslim, and he was steeped in both cultures. So I asked him if a practicing Muslim could dissociate the Sharia religious law from his faith in Islam. "Absolutely not," he replied. "Those are the laws of God."

So, I asked, "In today's world, we should cut off the hands of thieves?"

"That is God's law," he replied, "and it is a deterrent."

He had just made my point for me, and I told him so. He had lived for many years in England and he was British, but his archaic, brutal concept of justice and law ran much deeper than that. I knew better than to argue with him; there was no way I could reconcile the complete incompatibility—the clash of thought—that lay between us.

This is a small example of a larger issue, and one that is growing in importance. For years, the West didn't see it coming, but now, surely, we must, for it involves our society too. It has become impossible for fundamentalist Muslims to separate the Sharia code from their religious beliefs. For them it simply cannot be done, for the Sharia is an indissociable part of their religion. Any alternative point of view is unacceptable for these zealots, which is why democracy as we know it in the West may not be able to exist in the Muslim world. A fundamentalist cannot allow the ideas that he sees as his religious law to be subjected to scrutiny and debate.

In the West, our laws can be reviewed and changed to adapt to our modern world. An unjust and outdated law is questioned. It is noticed, resented, and fought about, sometimes bitterly. Ours is not a perfect society, but it has the strength and flexibility to examine itself and change. We look forward and we seek to improve our laws and our society. To Islamic fundamentalists, Sharia law is immutable. All society must be guided by the way the original community of Muslims in the seventh century lived and thought. Therefore everyone looks backward.

What I saw in Saudi Arabia was a culture that refused to evolve. After the tragedy of 9/11, Americans began to ask why they should be so hated. I think the issue goes deeper than Osama Bin Laden's hatred of America. I think he has a larger plan: to propagate what he and many others like him see as the "pure" form of Islam, and to establish it in the Muslim world and beyond, wherever he can.

Think of this: There are 1.2 billion Muslims in the world. Not all of them, by any means, are fanatics, and I do not mean to suggest that they are. But even assuming only ten percent of Muslims follow the strongest, most conservative precepts of Islam, that is 120 million people. Of that number, surely no more than ten percent are extremists. But that means 12 million people have been ideologically conditioned to impose their conservative conception of Islam on others. And perhaps ten percent of those extremists are so fanatical that they are prepared to die for their beliefs (because dying for them will earn them eternal paradise). This means that scattered all over the world, a shadow army more than one million people strong is primed to attack Western values and Western culture.

The de facto spearhead of this shadow army is my former brother-in-law, Osama Bin Laden. To those who long to obey his every whim, Osama is a hero; to the less zealous, he remains a charismatic figure, of a good Muslim.

Certain of his popularity among the faithful, Osama Bin Laden had the arrogance to release a video four days before the US presidential election. He confirmed that he had masterminded the 9/11 attacks, and blamed his barbaric action on American policy. He even had the nerve to advise Americans on "the best way to avoid another tragedy." He compared the American government to "a crocodile attacking a helpless child" and threatened to "bleed America." I was outraged. He dared to offend the victims' families by calling the attack that he instigated a "tragedy." But if he considered it tragic, then why did he do it? He admitted that he had ordered the violence, then acted as if it was someone else's fault—the fault of the victim. He never questioned the rightness of what he did, and showed no remorse for the people he murdered. I could only shake with rage.

Osama Bin Laden's attacks are not limited to America. On the morning of March 11, 2004, four bombs exploded on three crowded commuter trains in Spain's capital city of Madrid. At least 173 people were killed, and more than 400 were wounded. This horrible, heartless attack on innocent people heading to work bore the sign of Osama Bin Laden's twisted thinking. Like the others who share his views, he will stop at nothing.

Today the fundamentalists are more convinced than ever that they hold the real truth of Islam, and that it is their duty to show their fellow Muslims the true path. I say this with regret: I am convinced that their position won't change any time soon. I have also come to believe that you cannot change a country from the outside. The change must come from within.

Will Saudi women, for example, ever *want* the freedoms that Western women fought so hard to get? To overturn the laws in Saudi Arabia that deny women certain basic human rights, the women there would have to *want* freedom. They would have to fight for it. But in my years living among them, I saw no desire in Saudi Arabian women to change their situation.

In the twenty-first century, women everywhere should have the freedom to choose how they live their lives. In Saudi Arabia, it seems to me, most women would recoil at the idea of giving their daughters our kind of freedom. They would not want them to learn openness, equality, freedom of thought, or anything that might lead them to question their culture. Most Saudi women don't see the restrictions imposed on them as a repression of their personality. Many of them actually *choose* to remain under the guardianship of men, because they see it as protection. They embrace it, and they perpetuate it. They don't see the bars of the cages they are making for themselves and their children.

In Saudi Arabia, the deep-rooted and basic tenets of society are *never* questioned, for anything that is fundamental to Saudi society is based on religion, and religion cannot be doubted. Even the liberal, dissident Saudis—and there are some, both male and female—oppose only details. They demand only practical and convenient changes, such as the right to drive a car. They criticize aspects of the al-Saud regime: that it is corrupt, bloated, parasitical, unworthy in some way. But the real problems in Saudi Arabia go so much deeper. No government arising in that country today would be able to forgo the deep beliefs of Wahabi Islam.

We are thus at an impasse: our world, and theirs. They cannot change, and we must not. We should not allow them to use our tolerance to impose their intolerance on us. Today fundamentalists have the power to affect us in places they were previously unable to reach. They can strike us wherever they please. And I fear that this will continue, now and for as long as the powerful families of the oil kingdoms continue to feel it is either their moral duty or it is just politically useful for them to spend hundreds of millions of dollars to spread their beliefs.

As a young woman, I was naïvely confident that freedom would come soon to Saudi Arabia. Now I am no longer so sure. Because of my struggle for my daughters, I have thought so much about life in Saudi Arabia, about what I know of the characteristics of that society. And I ask myself the hardest question: How can we overcome such a violent clash of cultures?

Acknowledgments

I would like to express my deepest gratitude and love to:

My daughters, Wafah, Najia, and Noor, for their immeasurable courage and the strength and support they have shown me during those long years of struggle. In spite of the dark times that they have lived through, they have managed to become beautiful human beings.

My mother, who always made me feel loved and special, and whose courage has inspired me.

Mary Martha Barkley, who is always there for me. My life would have been much the poorer without her example.

Thomas, who lavishes love and unconditional support on my daughters.

Frédéric Marti, whose understanding, talent, and tenacity have enabled me to keep my girls.

Peter Lilley, who believed in me from our very first meeting.

Pierre Alain Schmidt, who has had the courage to defend me in my divorce case and to stand by me even when it seemed hopeless.

Working on this project has allowed me to meet two fantastic people, Susanna Lea and Ruth Marshall, whose patience and support have been invaluable. I know they will be part of my life forever.

And of course, I would like to express my special love and thanks to my friends, who have been there for me at even the most difficult times: Sabine and Matthias Kalina; Lois, John, and Shelton West; Ula Sabag; Géraldine, Ulrika, Carlos, and Guillaume.